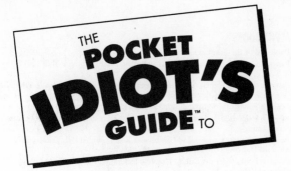

Texas Hold'em

by Randy Burgess and Carl Baldassarre

D1018627

ALPHA

A member of Penguin Group (USA) Inc.

ALPHA BOOKS

Published by the Penguin Group

Penguin Group (USA) Inc., 375 Hudson Street, New York, New York 10014, U.S.A.

Penguin Group (Canada), 10 Alcorn Avenue, Toronto, Ontario, Canada M4V 3B2 (a division of Pearson Penguin Canada Inc.)

Penguin Books Ltd, 80 Strand, London WC2R 0RL, England

Penguin Ireland, 25 St Stephen's Green, Dublin 2, Ireland (a division of Penguin Books Ltd)

Penguin Group (Australia), 250 Camberwell Road, Camberwell, Victoria 3124, Australia (a division of Pearson Australia Group Pty Ltd)

Penguin Books India Pvt Ltd, 11 Community Centre, Panchsheel Park, New Delhi—110 017, India

Penguin Group (NZ), cnr Airborne and Rosedale Roads, Albany, Auckland 1310, New Zealand (a division of Pearson New Zealand Ltd)

Penguin Books (South Africa) (Pty) Ltd, 24 Sturdee Avenue, Rosebank, Johannesburg 2196, South Africa

Penguin Books Ltd, Registered Offices: 80 Strand, London WC2R 0RL, England

Copyright © 2004 by Randy Burgess and Carl Baldassarre

International Standard Book Number: 1-59257-325-8
Library of Congress Catalog Card Number: 2004115234

07   06   05   8   7   6   5   4   3   2

Interpretation of the printing code: The rightmost number of the first series of numbers is the year of the book's printing; the rightmost number of the second series of numbers is the number of the book's printing. For example, a printing code of 04-1 shows that the first printing occurred in 2004.

Printed in the United States of America

Note: This publication contains the opinions and ideas of its authors. It is intended to provide helpful and informative material on the subject matter covered. It is sold with the understanding that the authors and publisher are not engaged in rendering professional services in the book. If the reader requires personal assistance or advice, a competent professional should be consulted.

The authors and publisher specifically disclaim any responsibility for any liability, loss, or risk, personal or otherwise, which is incurred as a consequence, directly or indirectly, of the use and application of any of the contents of this book.

Most Alpha books are available at special quantity discounts for bulk purchases for sales promotions, premiums, fund-raising, or educational use. Special books, or book excerpts, can also be created to fit specific needs.

For details, write: Special Markets, Alpha Books, 375 Hudson Street, New York, NY 10014.

Contents

Appendixes

Introduction

Hold'em poker is America's game. It's the game of the World Series of Poker in Las Vegas, and the game friends choose to play around the kitchen table. Now you can make it your game.

This guide teaches you everything you need to play Hold'em. And not just how to play, but to win. We've never played with anyone who doesn't like winning, so we're going to assume you'll enjoy it, too.

There's plenty to know about Hold'em, but learning how to play the game well isn't a subject reserved for cigar-smoking Texans or stone-faced young men in wraparound sunglasses. Hold'em is a great equalizer. In a home game, a computer technician can take a CEO's money. In the casino, a 60-year-old grandmother can outplay a flashy young gambler.

From the rules of the game to strategies every successful player needs to know, we've kept our explanations simple. You'll also find an introduction to places to play, the kinds of players you're likely to encounter, and different types of games from Internet poker to no-limit tournaments.

Although it might be hard to believe, many of your opponents won't take the time to read a book like this. We guarantee you an advantage over them, even if you've never played before in your life.

Using this Book

In addition to the main text, this book includes sidebars, each with a distinctive visual cue:

Talk Like a Texan _____

These sidebars include definitions of basic Hold'em terms.

Build Your Stack _____

These provide insights and side glimpses into poker lore and poker fact.

Raise It Up _____

These are playing tips that show you how strategize and win.

Watch Your Chips _____

These warnings tell you what to watch out for and how to avoid common mistakes.

We've also sprinkled quizzes throughout the book. Take these quizzes seriously—for example, cover up the answers and think about the questions before you read the answers—and you'll learn Hold'em even faster.

Acknowledgments

Both of us are grateful to Joe Bunevith, a.k.a. Joe Tall, for taking time away from the tables to review the strategy portions of this book. We also thank Thom Forbes, home-game honcho extraordinaire, Mike Sanders of Alpha Books, and our agent, Bob Diforio, for dealing us in on this project and giving us a shot at the big time.

In addition, Carl thanks Randy, his co-author, for being a good Hold'em player, a great writer, and an even better friend; and Marian, his wife, for her love and spirit—as well as for her extraordinary generosity in putting up with late nights spent playing Hold'em, and still more late nights writing about it.

Randy for his part admits that Carl, too, may be a good writer and friend—but what about all those leaks in his Hold'em game? Never mind that Carl's lifetime winnings are far bigger than Randy's. That's just variance!

On a somewhat more gracious note, Randy also thanks Katherine, Bob, and Celeste: The best part of poker is being able to leave the table and come back home to them.

Trademarks

All terms mentioned in this book that are known to be or are suspected of being trademarks or service marks have been appropriately capitalized. Alpha Books and Penguin Group (USA) Inc. cannot attest to the accuracy of this information. Use of a term in this book should not be regarded as affecting the validity of any trademark or service mark.

Chapter 1

Sit On Down, Pardner

In This Chapter

- Why play Hold'em?
- Where to find games
- Hold'em myths vs. the real deal
- Achieving your goals

Corky McQuorcodale, a traveling poker player, is widely credited with having brought a new form of poker to Las Vegas in 1963. Known as Texas Hold'em—or just plain Hold'em—the game's popularity spread over the next four decades.

Now it's not only the most popular form of poker in the world, it's the most popular of *all time*. As you read this, millions are playing it in casinos, clubs, home games, and on the Internet. And the odds are, you picked up this book because you play Hold'em already and want to improve, or you want to learn how to get started.

Whether you're into the game or still undecided, in this chapter we'll put all the cards on the table and take a look at the forces behind the Texas Hold'em boom.

Why Play Hold'em?

Of course, you have your own good reasons for wanting to learn Hold'em, but there could be a couple more that you haven't thought of. This section describes four of the best, as we see them.

Reason 1: It's Fun

Hey, it's a game! If you enjoy board or card games, you'll like Hold'em. And there are additional pleasures, depending on your setting. If you're playing a good home game, the insults, banter, and sociability can be as entertaining as the cards. In a casino, you can enjoy the swank feel of genuine green felt, the hefty, custom-designed clay chips, and the luxury of ordering food or drink without leaving your seat.

Reason 2: It's Easy

Even if you've never played Hold'em before, you can get started in just a few minutes. The next chapter explains the rules quickly and simply. Read it, deal out a few practice hands, review the strategy tips in the rest of this book, and you'll be ready to play.

Build Your Stack

Texas Hold'em may not have even origi-
nated in Texas! Early forms of poker,
based on century-old European card
games, were first played in New Orleans
in the early 1800s. As poker moved north-
ward on the Mississippi with riverboat
gamblers, draw, five-card stud, and seven-
card stud emerged as popular variations.
Hold'em didn't even originate until some-
time around 1900, poker historians specu-
late. Why it remained virtually unknown
for so long is still a mystery.

Reason 3: It's Challenging

This may sound like a direct contradiction to
Reason 2, but rest assured it isn't. While the basics
of Hold'em are easy to learn, playing at a high level
can take years of thought and study.

According to experts in both games, Hold'em and
bridge are comparable in difficulty. Some even say
Hold'em is as demanding as chess. (In fact, many
young American grandmasters these days also play
Hold'em!)

However, mastery of Hold'em requires a different
combination of skills than other games. The best
players rely on a unique combination of mathemat-
ics, psychology, and card sense.

Finally, Hold'em is challenging because you can keep raising the stakes. At each higher level, both the pressure and the relative skill of your opponents increase, too. After all, it's a lot different playing for millions of dollars in a nationally televised tournament than playing for quarters around the kitchen table.

This is to your advantage. When you're starting out, you can find a level of play that you're comfortable with and stick with it as long as you like. There's no pressure, and if you start to get bored, you can always find some new and interesting aspect of the game to work on. Any time you want to move up to more challenging levels and stakes, new games and players will be waiting for you.

Reason 4: It Can Make You Money

If you play Hold'em regularly, you'll encounter fellow players who treat poker as if luck determines all, just as it does in casino games like roulette, craps, or keno.

They're wrong. As of now, you are officially on notice: winning at Hold'em relies on skill more than luck in the long run. That's why there are professional players in poker, but not roulette.

The great majority of Hold'em players lose money no matter how long they play. But, though exact figures are hard to come by, hundreds or even thousands of Hold'em players make a living at the game. In addition, an even greater number of players rely on their winnings to supplement income from other sources.

This guide can help you become one of the winners. But this doesn't mean that making a buck should be your primary reason to learn the game. Unless you turn out to be a poker prodigy, the time you invest in the game might be more profitably spent working or developing marketable skills for use outside the world of poker.

Still, a hobby that could potentially pay for itself is a pretty good deal. And the excitement of winning can be just as great even when the amounts involved are small.

Raise It Up

Just how often can a good player win at Hold'em? Excluding tournaments and no-limit Hold'em, a common benchmark is one bet per hour. So if you're playing in a casino or club game where the top bet is four dollars, you'd be doing well to average that much for each hour of play. Really strong players target 1.5 bets per hour. Online, where play is faster, winning between two and three bets for every 100 hands is roughly comparable.

Places to Play

Hold'em has never been more popular than it is right now. When you're ready to play, you can find a game in plenty of places. Here's a quick look at the pros and cons of your main choices.

Home Games

Most people first learn to play poker in home games. It's hard to beat the relaxed pace of play, the small stakes, and the chance to socialize and learn with friends.

Many home games are "dealer's choice." That means it's likely you'll play some Hold'em along with other forms of poker, like 7-card stud, Omaha, or draw. Some players may want to include wild-card games or other exotic variants.

To keep the game friendly, many home games deliberately keep the stakes low. Although good for sociability, this also encourages players to stay in for nearly every hand. This can keep you from learning the tactics necessary for winning in games that are even slightly less congenial.

If only you are serious about playing well, you'll probably be a consistent winner. After awhile, you may want to hone your skills against other serious players. If so, we suggest you look for a casino, cardroom, or Internet poker site. You can still play in your friendly home game when you're in the mood.

Casinos

Casinos are a great place to learn Hold'em. Many have a separate poker room, whether it's an actual room or a section of the main floor, populated by table after table of experienced players. Don't let that intimidate you. Welcoming newcomers is good business, so some casinos offer practice tables and most have plenty of low-stakes tables. While the game may seem confusing during your first few games, most dealers are patient with new players. With the growing popularity of the game, you probably won't be the only beginner.

 Build Your Stack

One tip: Many casinos don't offer poker of any kind. To avoid disappointment, call ahead of time to ask if there's a poker room and if they spread Hold'em at stakes you're comfortable with.

Cardrooms and Clubs

A large cardroom offers an experience similar to a casino. The biggest difference is that cardrooms typically have fewer nonpoker games than casinos. Some have only poker, while others sustain other card games as well.

Cardrooms are common in some states, notably California. Their size ranges from immense "card barns" with dozens of tables to tiny, single-table establishments.

In places where cardrooms aren't legal, underground poker clubs often spring up. The movie *Rounders* depicted several fictitious clubs in New York City.

Although the clubs in that movie were dramatic and menacing, real illegal clubs can be safe and pleasant places to play, much like chess, bridge, or backgammon clubs. If you play in an area where such clubs exist, you'll probably hear about one at some point. If you decide to go, be aware that there's a chance the club could be raided by police. In most states, playing isn't against the law, so only the club operators are subject to arrest. But you should check the law in your area before you play. It's also probably wise to bring a friend the first time you visit, and be ready to leave if anything about the club or the other players makes you uncomfortable.

The Internet

Cyberspace is currently the most popular place to play Hold'em. On a single night, more than 10,000 cardsharks can gather for Hold'em at one of the more popular Internet sites. No casino or cardroom in the world can come close to matching those staggering numbers. And remember, that's just one site of dozens.

Of course, many people love the sociability of a live game and the feel of real cards and chips. But many others prefer the convenience of having a game available wherever there's a computer and an

Internet connection. For those who don't live near a place to play, the Internet offers the only game in town.

There are many reasons to like online poker, especially if you're a beginner. For one thing, the online poker sites have low overhead, so they can offer *much* lower stakes than you'll find anywhere else. It's commonplace to find Hold'em games where the maximum bet is 25¢ or 50¢, for example. Many sites also offer play money games, if you want to get your feet wet without risking even a mild soaking.

Online play allows you to learn the game at an accelerated pace. In a casino you might see 35 hands an hour, whereas online you'll typically see at least 80. So if you're comfortable using a computer, you get twice as many chances per hour to improve your game.

Having listed the advantages of Internet Hold'em, we'd be remiss if we didn't mention one potential drawback: running an Internet poker site is illegal in the United States. All the major sites are based offshore.

With advertisements on television and on the Internet, the big poker sites certainly aren't hiding what they are doing. Neither are many players— people continue to play openly in homes, offices, and Internet cafes. While it's likely that there will be attempts to regulate the free-wheeling world of Internet poker in the future, most players appear to be simply ignoring the issue at present.

Watch Your Chips

Poker is a social game—and yet you'll often hear players complain about their luck, berate the dealer, or criticize their opponents for making "stupid" plays. Smart players don't act this way, and you shouldn't either. Channel your aggressive instincts into playing your hardest, not taking a hard-nosed attitude. You'll have a better time and you'll probably play better if you're not distracted by frustration or anger.

Make-Believe vs. the Real Deal

We've already touched on one of the most common misconceptions about Hold'em—the notion that luck trumps skill. If most of your poker experience has been watching movies like *Rounders* or televised tournaments such as the World Series of Poker, you may have few other misguided notions, too. Let's debunk these before going any further to make sure they don't cost you bets at the table.

- **Make-Believe: Hold'em is an action game where you play lots of hands.** The dealer deals out the cards, the camera zooms in, and the chips start to fly. What else is there?

- **The Real Deal: Hold'em involves a lot of sitting and waiting.** It's not exciting and the cameras don't dwell on it, but a good Hold'em player spends far more time folding his first two cards than playing them. This is true even in tournaments, where various gimmicks such as stack-devouring antes force you to play many more hands than normal. As you'll find out in the next few chapters, it pays to be picky.

- **Make-Believe: You have to bluff a lot.** In both movies and televised tournaments, the combatants frequently win huge pots with bold bluffs. Even though you're just starting out, you may be thinking you can do the same.

- **The Real Deal: At low limits, you should rarely bluff.** Those big bluffers are playing no-limit Hold'em, where calling a bluff can cost someone his entire stack of chips. But most of this book is about playing limit Hold'em, where the small bet size means that bluffs are usually called and the best hand takes the pot. We'll get to bluffing in the chapters on tournaments and advanced play, but for now, leave it out of your repertoire.

- **Make-Believe:** You'll often have to outplay a single opponent. Just as in *Rounders*, you and John Malkovich head-up, right?

- **The Real Deal: You'll usually have many opponents.** Put your Matt Damonesque fantasies aside: at most low-limit Hold'em tables, it's common to reach the showdown with several opponents, with only an occasional head-up confrontation. You'll rely less on bluffing than on playing strategies that do well against a crowd.

Setting Your Sights

So why exactly *do* people play Hold'em? We went over the reasons before, but this section describes a few real-life examples.

One player is an engineer at a large company who plays Hold'em more than 25 hours a week. He's a former college athlete, very competitive, and regularly plays for big stakes in games that often include professional players. His main goals are to constantly improve his game and to win money to supplement his income.

Another player successfully freelances as a writer. He's a consistent winner in low-stakes games, even though work and a growing family allow him time to play only a few hours a week. His main goals are to pursue an enjoyable hobby while slowly building his skills and his winnings.

Finally, we've read about a highly successful software executive who occasionally takes time away from the office to play low-stakes Hold'em.

Reports suggest he probably doesn't play enough to be a consistent winner, but we doubt he minds losing a few dollars. That man is Bill Gates, the founder of Microsoft. We have no way of knowing for sure, but we'd guess his goal might be simply to spend a few hours relaxing.

Now it's your turn. Before you invest any more time or money in the game, decide what you want to receive in return. Relaxation? Money? Sociability? Competition? Mental stimulation? Winning the World Series of Poker?

By setting goals right from the start, you'll create a way to assess how you're doing as your Hold'em game evolves and improves.

The Least You Need to Know

- Hold'em is a form of poker that's recently become the most popular variation of the game.
- Skill is more important than luck. In the long run, a good player wins consistently.
- You can play Hold'em at home with friends, in casinos and cardrooms, and on the Internet.
- Luck, bluffing, and fancy one-on-one moves are much less important than most new Hold'em players think.

Chapter 2

Hold'em Basics

In This Chapter

- Ranking of hands
- Dealing Hold'em
- How the betting works
- Reading the board and examples

May the Best Five Cards Win

Before you begin learning the strategies and tactics that make winning Hold'em so much fun, you need to know the absolute basics. By the end of this chapter, you'll understand how the cards are dealt, how the betting works, and a little bit more besides. We're not talking mastery here, just enough to get you started. First, let's make sure you're ready. If you haven't played a lick of poker in your life, you'll need to acquaint yourself with the most fundamental poker concept of all—what makes a winning hand. If you already know this, you can skip ahead.

Five might be the most important number in poker, if only because five cards make a complete poker hand. This is true no matter how many cards you're dealt, whether seven, as in seven-card-stud, or just two, as in Hold'em. (Hmm, how can you make a five-card hand if you're only dealt two cards? We'll solve that mystery in a page or two.)

This leads us to our next topic: the ranking of the different possible hands. Not coincidentally, they're ranked by how often they occur. Hard-to-get hands are top dog, while everyday mongrels command little respect. For example, if you deal out five-card hands to yourself from a shuffled deck, you'll average getting a pair every other hand. On the other hand, three-of-a-kind will come along just once every 34 hands. Take a gander at the table and then let's talk about it.

Rank of Poker Hands

Name	Example	Ways to Get	Odds Against if This Hand Dealt 5 Cards
Royal flush	A♦ K♦ Q♦ J♦ T♦	4	649,739 to 1
Straight flush	8♠ 7♠ 6♠ 5♠ 4♠	36	64,973 to 1
Four of a kind	7777 5	624	3,913 to 1
Full house	333 KK	3,744	589 to 1
Flush	J♥ 9♥ 5♥ 4♥ 2♥	5,108	272 to 1
Straight	JT987	10,200	131 to 1
Three of a kind	888 A K	54,912	34 to 1
Two pair	77 66 Q	123,552	12 to 1
One pair	JJ A 9 3	1,098,240	Even
No pair	K T 9 8 7	1,302,540	

You'll see that in Hold'em poker, a Ten is abbreviated not as 10, but T. More obviously, an Ace is abbreviated as A, a King as K, and so on for the face cards. Cards from 9 down are simply referred to by number. We'll talk about some additional abbreviations in Chapter 4.

Here are some additional fine points on determining the best hand:

- **If more than one player has a full house,** the highest ranking three-of-a-kind wins. For example, QQQ 22 beats 444 AA.

- **Between competing flushes or competing straights,** the high card determines the winner: for example, a Jack-high straight beats a Ten-high straight. For flushes only, if the top card is a tie, the next card counts, and so on, down to the last card: for example, AQ983 beats AQ982.

- **If more than one player has two pair,** the highest pair wins. For example, AA 22 beats KK QQ. If two players both have the same two pair, then the fifth card counts: AA 22 5 beats AA 22 3.

- **If nobody has a pair,** the winner is the player holding the highest card. If there's a tie you can go all the way down to the last card, just as with two battling flushes.

- **In the case of a tie in every respect,** the players split the pot.

Raise It Up

As you learn the ranking of the hands, remember that a small hand like Ace-high can win a lot of money if it's the *best* hand at the time. And a big hand like a straight flush may win only peanuts if no other big hands are around to contest it. Always remember, value in poker is relative, not absolute.

Dealing the Cards

To start with, each player is dealt two cards face down. These cards are known as *hole cards*, and in Hold'em, they're the only cards that are yours alone. A round of betting follows. Next, the dealer *burns* the top card in the deck—that is, he discards it sight-unseen, face down on the table. Now he deals three cards face up in the center of the table. This is the *flop*. These three cards are community cards, meaning everyone can use them. There's another round of betting.

The dealer now deals a fourth face-up card, called the *turn*. Again, it's a shared card that all players can use, and again, it's followed by a round of betting. A fifth and final card is dealt face-up, called the *river*. There's one last round of betting. If more than one player is left in the hand, there's a show-down: the players flip over their hole cards to see who has the best hand. The five cards in the middle are collectively called the *board*. Each player gets to combine one, both, or none of his hole cards with any of the cards from the board to create his best five-card poker hand.

Talk Like a Texan

To **burn** means to discard the top card from the deck, face down. In Hold'em, the dealer does this before dealing the flop, the turn, and the river as well. Why? Ostensibly, it's to prevent cheating—for example, if any of the cards have been marked or scuffed in a way that makes them identifiable. Although such caution is usually unnecessary, burning is a hallowed Hold'em tradition.

You Can't Bet the Moon

Let's turn our attention to the essence of poker—betting. The first thing to know is how *much* you can bet. The answer isn't "how thick is your wallet?" but "what's the betting structure?" There are four basic structures:

- **No-limit.** This is what they play at the World Series of Poker. You can bet just one chip or your entire stack of chips at any point in the hand. We'll talk more about this in Chapter 10.

- **Pot-limit.** The pot is the money in the middle of the table—so when we say pot-limit, we mean you can bet or raise any amount up to the total amount in the pot. Like no-limit, pot-limit is a game for experienced players.

- **Spread-limit.** Limit poker means exactly that: bets and raises are limited to a set amount, generally smaller than the pot. In spread-limit, you can bet or raise any amount between a minimum and maximum. For example, in $1-$3 spread-limit, a common beginner game at many casinos, you can bet anywhere from $1-$3 at any time. The only qualification is that a raise must be at least as big as the preceding bet.

- **Structured limit.** This is the most common betting structure outside of tournaments, and the one we'll be referring to most often in this book. Bets before the flop and on the flop are one amount, and bets on the turn and river are exactly double this amount. For example, in $3-$6 structured limit, bets or raises before the flop and on the flop are $3, and bets and raises on the turn and river are $6.

Betting Blind

While we're on the subject of betting, remember that all forms of poker require some money go into the pot before any cards are dealt. Otherwise, there'd be nothing to play for and everyone would sit tight until they got perfect cards.

Games like seven-card stud or five-card draw seed the pot by requiring each player to contribute a fraction of a bet, called an *ante*. Hold'em is also played this way in some home games.

Casinos or clubs, however, use a different method for Hold'em: Two players are required to contribute blind bets to the pot, or *blinds*. In a limit game, the player who is the *big blind* must contribute a bet equal to the limit, while the *little blind* must contribute either $\frac{1}{3}$, $\frac{1}{2}$, or $\frac{2}{3}$ of a bet.

Obviously, it's a handicap to have to put money into the pot without seeing your cards first. To ensure everyone takes their turn, a plastic disc that looks a little like a white hockey puck is moved clockwise around the table, one position with each deal. This disk is called the *dealer button*. The player who has the button is called either the *button*, or the *dealer*, regardless of the fact that there's a professional dealer doing the actual handing out of cards.

The little blind sits to the immediate left of the dealer button, and the big blind sits two seats to the left. This way everyone pays his or her dues as big and little blind, and everyone gets a chance to be dealer.

Putting Cards and Betting Together

You're just about ready to play along with some
sample hands. But first, let's look at how the cards,
the blinds, and the betting work together.

Before the Flop

Before any cards are dealt, the big and little blinds
put forward their blind bets. It's proper etiquette to
place these chips in front of you, rather than toss
them directly into the pot. The dealer will gather
them up once the betting is done for the round.

Now the dealer gives everyone his or her hole
cards. These are yours alone to look at, and it
actually matters how you go about this. To avoid
flashing a card, seasoned Hold'em players never
pick the hole cards up off the table. Instead, bring
your two cards neatly together, still face down,
then cup your hands over them and use a thumb
to peel up the ends nearest you—just enough for
you to see what you've got, and no one else.

Betting begins with the player seated to the immediate left of the big blind, or *under the gun*. This
player can *call* the blind bet by placing chips to
match in front of him, or *fold*, in which case
he surrenders his cards by pushing them face
down toward the dealer. If he likes his hand,
however, he can also *raise*. For example, in a $3-$6
structured-limit game, he could raise the big blind's
$3 bet by another $3, making the total bet $6.

Watch Your Chips _____

There's a rule in clubs and casinos that if you don't protect your hole cards, they can be rendered unplayable if another player throws away his or her cards and those cards touch yours. You can also lose your cards if the dealer accidentally gathers them as he's collecting other players' folded hands. Fortunately, protecting your hand is easy: After you've looked at your cards, and hopefully memorized them, place a chip or a coin on top of them.

The betting continues clockwise. Each player in turn chooses to call, fold, or raise. In most games, the number of raises is limited to three or four per betting round. The exception is when only two players are involved, in which case casinos and clubs usually permit an unlimited number of raises.

When the action gets around to the little blind, she, too, must call, fold, or raise. In any case, she has already paid a fraction of a bet, so it is cheaper for her to call than for the other players. If she folds, she forfeits her blind.

The big blind is last to act before the flop. He's got the same options as the players before him, with one difference: Because he's already put in a full bet, if no one has raised and he himself doesn't want to raise, he can simply *check*, indicating he's taking no further action. He does this either by saying "check" or by rapping the table.

> **Raise It Up**
>
> If you've got the dealer button before the flop and everyone in front of you folds, you can consider raising even with mediocre cards. Your goal is to "steal" the blinds, by folding all of the remaining players.
>
> Occasionally, everyone will fold to the little blind. In that case the big blind and little blind can either play it out, or else agree to take back their blinds. The latter practice is known as *chopping,* and it can save you from being penalized by the ominous-sounding *rake.* For more on the rake, see Chapter 9.

On the Flop

After the three common cards of the flop are dealt, betting starts again. This time, whoever is immediately to the left of the dealer leads off. If the little blind called the bet before the flop, this will be her. Because in this round no one has bet yet, she has the option of checking, meaning she takes no action, or betting.

The betting action keeps moving to the left. If the first player checked, the next player has the same options of either checking or betting. But if the first player bet, the next player must now either call that bet, fold, or raise.

The action continues around the table, until either everyone has checked, or someone has opened the betting and gotten at least one caller (or possibly a raiser). If everyone checks, then everyone remains in and gets to see the turn card. But if someone bets, only those players who call that bet (or raise it) get to see the turn card. Otherwise, they must fold. If no one calls, the bettor wins the pot right there.

Of course, once someone puts in the first bet, all other players are free to not merely call but raise—with additional raises possible after that, until the maximum of three or four has been reached. Once again, there must be at least one caller of a raise or reraise for the action to proceed to the next stage. If not, the raiser or reraiser wins the pot right there.

On the Turn and River

Betting on the turn and the river is just like on the flop. In each case, the first remaining player to the left of the dealer button is first to act.

On the river, if more than one player is left in the hand after the betting is over, the players flip over their hands. This is called the *showdown*. The dealer pushes the pot to the winner, or if there's a tie, he splits the pot accordingly. The button is moved one position to the left, the dealer shuffles the cards, and we start all over again.

> **Raise It Up** _____
>
> You may have noticed that the player with the dealer button gets to act last on the flop, turn, and river. If that seemed like an advantage, congratulations—you're on your way to becoming a winning Hold'em player!
>
> Being last to act is called having **position**, and is indeed an edge. You get to see what everyone else does and act accordingly, while they can only guess at what you'll do. We'll talk more about the importance of position in further chapters.

Let's Play!

We're ready for our example hands. You can just read along, but it wouldn't hurt to get out a deck of cards and deal them out to match the example. It's like learning to speak a foreign language— the more realistic you can make it, the faster it'll sink in.

Example One

Hold'em can be played with as few as two players, in which case we say they're playing *head-up* or *heads-up*, to as many as ten, which we call a *ring game*.

To keep things simple for our example, we'll have just four players: Larry, Moe, Joe, and Sally. This is sometimes called a *short-handed* game, as compared to a ring game.

Let's get to our action.

Pre-Flop

Sally had the dealer button for the hand before, so now it slides over to Larry. It's a $3-$6 limit game, so Moe posts a little blind of $1, and Joe posts a big blind of $3. Now the players get their cards.

Remember that before the flop, it's not the big and little blind who act first, but the player who is to their immediate left—the player under the gun. In this case, it's Sally. She loves her Ace-King combo. It's a powerful hand, so she raises, putting forward $6 in chips.

Larry takes one look at the dreck he's been dealt and *mucks* it, pushing the cards face down toward the dealer. He'll rarely win a pot with Q8 offsuit (unsuited), so he's better off just watching.

Moe and Joe have decent hands, however, so they both call the raise. Moe puts in $5 in addition to his $1 blind, and Joe puts in $3.

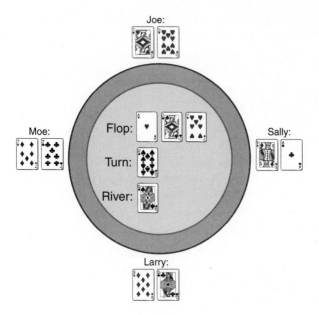

Example One

Flop

Stop! Before you read on, stop and look at the table, then work out for yourself what each active player now holds for his or her best five-card poker hand.

Ready? Let's resume the action.

Moe, the little blind, is excited: he's flopped what in Hold'em parlance is called a *set*—three-of-a-kind, with two of the three cards being his hole cards. This is a very powerful hand, and so Moe unhesitatingly bets the limit of $3.

Joe, the big blind, likes his hand, too, so he calls the bet. He's flopped *second pair*, meaning the second-best possible pair hand, with his pair of Jacks. In addition he has a flush *draw*—either of the two cards to come can give him a flush in Hearts. Stop and work it out if you don't see it.

Meanwhile, Sally has flopped a pair of Aces. Her second-best card is the King from her hole cards. If someone else had also flopped a pair of Aces, but held a smaller kicker, Sally would likely be winning because of her King. You'll read more about kickers in the next chapter. In any case, Sally likes her *top pair* so much she raises, making the bet $6.

With his powerful set, Moe could reraise—but he knows that in this structured-limit game, the bet size doubles on the next card. He decides to set a trap for Sally by just calling here.

Turn

Again, stop and look at the table and work out the player's best five-card hands for yourself, now that they each have six cards to work with. Moe's hand hasn't gotten any better, but it hasn't gotten any worse: it's still quite strong. But strangely, he checks. Joe's hand *has* improved: He still has his flush draw, but the Ten on the turn gives him two pair, Jacks and Tens. He bets $6. Sally is worried that top pair might not be the best hand anymore, but she calls anyway. The action is back to Moe, and now he springs his trap—he raises! Both Joe and Sally are forced to call his *check-raise* so they can continue.

River

What does everyone have now? Sally doesn't hold back—she bets $6. Moe raises, still confident, and Joe gives up and folds. Sally reraises and Moe realizes his hand may not be best after all and just calls.

When the smoke clears, Sally has the best possible hand with her Ace-high straight, Moe has the second-best hand with his set of Sevens, and Joe was smart to fold his third-best hand of Jacks and Tens. Sally takes down a $108 pot.

Example Two

There's no betting this time—just read the boards and the hole cards as shown in the tables, then figure out each player's best five-card poker hand and the ultimate winner.

Joe is the lowest hand, with only his pair of Aces in the hole. Sally easily beats Joe with a full house, Kings full of Tens; but Larry beats Sally just as easily with *quads*, or four-of-a-kind. Larry in turn loses to the winner, Moe, for whom the river card made a King-high straight flush.

Remember that in Hold'em, you can use one, both, or none of your hole cards in combination with the board. In this case, Moe needed only the J♠ in his hand to make the winner.

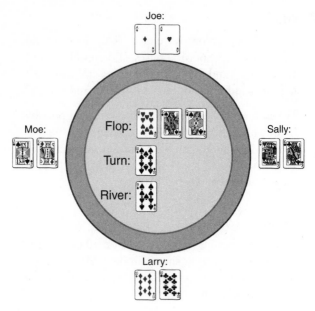

Example Two

Example Three

Here, Joe flopped top pair with his Ace, and his Queen gave him a good *kicker*, or side card. But Joe's hand never improves, and winds up as the worst hand of the four.

Sally makes a set of Fours on the turn, but fails to improve to either a full house or quads on the river, either of which would probably have won. Her hand beats Joe's, but isn't the winner.

Moe flops a Five-high straight, and probably feels he should win—but he has the bad luck to get *counterfeited* when cards fall on the turn and the river that match his hand but don't improve it. These cards give Larry a Six-high straight using the Six in his hand, making him the winner.

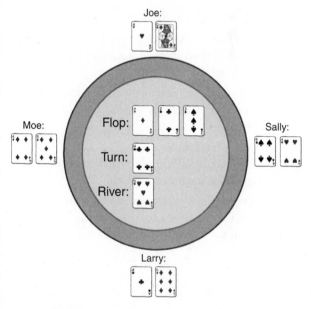

Example Three

What Next, Tex?

Judging the relative strength of your hand versus the best possible hand is an acquired skill. We recommend you get a deck of cards and start dealing out five-card boards—flop, turn, and river. Skip the hole cards for now.

For each board, figure out the best possible hand, the second best, and so on. The best hand is called the *nuts*. A good Hold'em player can recognize the nuts, second nuts, and third nuts in a glance. Don't stop practicing until you can do the same. It's cheaper to learn this way than in an actual game!

The Least You Need to Know

- The dealer gives each player two hole cards; everyone then shares a three-card flop, a turn card, and a river card.

- You make your best five-card poker hand from your hole cards and the five shared cards.

- Structured-limit is the most common form of Hold'em outside of tournaments, and the easiest for beginners to learn.

- Betting moves clockwise, and always begins with the player immediately to the left of the dealer button.

Chapter 3

What Do You Expect?

In This Chapter

- Hold'em math 101
- Simplifying things with odds and outs
- Drawing hands, made hands, and trash hands

Naturally, we're going to give you a lot of advice on how to win in the chapters to come—but there's one key idea you have to absorb first. It's not a specific strategy or secret, but an underlying method for determining the value of different plays.

Many Hold'em players have no way to look back on a hand and decide if they played it right or wrong. You will. This chapter gives you a way to evaluate strategies objectively, and adapt them to different situations.

The method goes by the somewhat scary name of *mathematical expectation*. But don't get intimidated; if you made it through sixth grade, you'll do fine. It's the concepts that are critical, not the calculating.

No Math = No Chips

Let's agree that *something* has got to guide your decision-making in poker. The question is, what? Beginning players and long-time losers often fall back on seemingly plausible strategies such as these:

- **Win as many pots as possible.** If you win most of the pots, you'll win most of the money. It stands to reason, right?

- **Play as many hands as you can.** You can't win a pot if you're not in the hand.

- **Decide which cards to play based on how they've worked out before.** You raise with pocket Aces and lose, and decide never to raise with Aces again. Or you call with 72 and flop a full house, and decide 72 is an under-appreciated gem.

Each of these approaches is incorrect and riddled with false assumptions. Following them will only cost you chips. We'll have to look elsewhere.

Expectation to the Rescue

Remember that as complicated as Hold'em can seem, there are only five things you can ever do: check, fold, call, bet, or raise. That's it. So whatever we rely on, it should apply to each of these possible choices.

Just as skilled players reject the phony logic we've just examined, they also reject gut reactions like

"Holy cow, I've got three-of-a-kind—I'd better raise!" Instead, what they weigh is something as hard and cold as cash itself: in each and every situation that comes up, which choice will win the most money over the long run?

That's mathematical expectation in a nutshell. But let's get just a tad more specific.

When a check, fold, call, bet, or raise loses money, we say it has *negative expectation*; when it wins money, we say it has *positive expectation*. In nearly every case, the good Hold'em player chooses the action that will maximize his positive expectation or minimize his negative expectation. For example, although a fold can never have positive expectation in the sense of winning money, it can still be your best choice if it minimizes the amount of money you lose on this particular hand.

Raise It Up

Why do we say that in "nearly every case" we want positive expectation? Why not in every case? As it happens, some clever opponents are very good at figuring out our hole cards if we always play correctly. To fool them, we can misplay a few hands—for example, raising with a hand we'd normally throw away. By sowing confusion, we hope to gain more long-term than we lose short-term. See Chapter 7 for more.

Expectation by the Numbers

It's not quite enough to describe expectation verbally; as promised, we need to do a little math.

Put simply, if you stand to win D dollars if an event occurs that has the probability P, but nothing otherwise, your expectation is D times P. Here's an example: Say you expect to win a $100 pot half the time. Probabilities are always expressed as fractions of 1, so we write 50 percent or ½ as .5. If we also say that E stands for expectation, we arrive at a very simple equation:

$100 \times .5 = E$

If we do the math, we find that your expectation in this case is $50. End of math!

Does this mean that you'll always win $50 each time this situation comes up? Absolutely not. You'll win $100 about half the time, and nothing most other times. A few hands will end in ties, and you'll split the pot. We can't predict which times you'll win and which times you won't—that's where luck enters in. What we *can* say is that over the long run, your results will come nearer and nearer to that $50 ideal.

Raise It Up

Keep in mind that in poker, "the long run" can mean hundreds of thousands of hands. That's why players who decide which hands to play based on recent experience are making a mistake: Statistics show that pocket Aces are the best hole cards in Hold'em, but in the short term, you can lose with them many times in a row.

Using Expectation at the Table

Okay, so you've learned this great poker concept. How do you actually make use of it? Do you sit there at the poker table like Einstein, doing math in your head?

Not the way you might think. In the heat of battle, even a professional poker player rarely resorts to the type of math we've just shown. Such equations quickly get too complicated to solve when juggling chips and cards in real time.

And when you're first starting out, you won't be doing math at the table of *any* kind. It's just too much to handle. That's why in the chapters to come, we'll give you rules of thumb to follow, not equations.

Good players follow these rules of thumb, too. What's important to remember is that such rules are based not only on what has worked for good players in the past, but upon an understanding of mathematical expectation. Someone else has done the math so that you don't have to.

Having said all this, good Hold'em players frequently *do* make some rough-and-ready calculations about expectation at the table. But they do so using a much more convenient style of math. Let's take a peek.

Oddly Enough

You're already familiar with odds from everyday conversation: "The odds are pretty bad." "It's a million to one against them finishing in time." "Odds are she'll get the promotion."

Odds are just a shorthand way of stating the relative chances of a favorable or unfavorable outcome for a given number of events. You get the total number of events by adding together the favorable and unfavorable outcomes.

Let's use a nonpoker example first. Say you think the odds are 2 to 1 against it raining today. What you're really saying is that for every three days like today, it won't rain on two of those days and it will rain on one of them.

Translate this to poker: you're on the river with just one opponent. The pot is $10, and now your opponent bets $10, making the total pot $20. You have to decide whether in the long run you'll make or lose money by calling that $10 bet—that is, whether calling gives you positive or negative expectation. How do you go about it?

Pot Odds

To figure out your expectation, we need to first introduce another key concept: *pot odds*. Pot odds are computed by comparing the money that has already been placed in the pot to the size of the bet to us. In this case, our pot odds are the $20 in the pot to the $10 bet, or 2 to 1.

Now here's the reason pot odds are so important: We can compare them to the odds of our winning, and presto!—we're back to knowing whether our expectation will be positive or negative. It's that simple.

Raise It Up

Pot odds exist to get compared to other odds. To make such comparison easier, it's good to get in the habit of converting denominators to 1. Say we're contemplating a $70 pot and a $30 bet: instead of leaving our pot odds as 7 to 3, we can guesstimate them as just under 2.5 to 1. (The exact answer is 2⅓ to 1, but you'll rarely require such precision.)

In this case, let's say we think our chances of winning that $20 pot are 3 to 1 against. So once out of every four times we'll win $20, and the other three times we'll lose $10, for a combined loss of $30. That means a $10 loss overall. On average, we're losing $2.50 each time—definitely a negative expectation.

On the other hand, if our chances of winning are 2 to 1 against, we'll make $20 once out of every three times and lose $10 twice, breaking exactly even. We can call or not call as we choose and it won't make any difference in the long run.

And if our chances of winning are better than 2 to 1—say, dead even at 1 to 1—we've got a guaranteed long-term winner on our hands. For every two tries, we'll win that $20 pot once and lose our $10 bet once, giving us a positive expectation of $10 each time we call.

Outs and Odds

But just how do we go about calculating our chances of winning in the first place? If we don't have that number, we won't have anything to compare against our pot odds.

In some cases, math isn't the most important factor in assessing where you stand. When you're head-to-head with a single foe, the winning hand could be a monster or a mouse (though mice are far more common). In such cases, psychology, intuition, and logic help more than math in gauging your chances.

But it's different when you're drawing to a hand such as a straight, flush, or a full house, especially against many opponents. Such hands are usually powerful enough to give us confidence that if we catch the right cards on the turn or river, we'll win; if not, we'll probably lose. So all we need is a way to figure the odds of making our draw.

Here's a common example. Let's say your hole cards are the Ace and Eight of Hearts. The flop and turn put two Hearts on board, so if the river is a Heart, you'll make an Ace-high flush. Let's further say that you're confident a flush of any sort will win, let alone an Ace-high. So what are your chances?

It's surprisingly easy to calculate. You've seen six cards—your two hole cards and the four cards making up the flop and turn. That leaves 46 unseen cards in the deck. You've also seen four Hearts—the two on board and the two in your hand. That leaves nine Hearts left out of the 13 in the deck; these potentially winning cards are your *outs*.

Assuming you'll lose if you *don't* make the flush, your chances of winning now become 37 to 9, or 5.1 against. You can now compare this to your pot odds: Let's say the pot contains $40 and the bet to you is $10—if you don't figure to make any more money on the river, you should fold, since your 5-to-1 odds of making the flush are worse than your 4-to-1 pot odds.

Talk Like a Texan

Outs in Hold'em are the number of cards that you think will make you a winning hand. **Tainted outs** are as insidious as they sound—cards that give you a good hand, but make your opponent a better hand: a heart that gives you a flush might make someone else a full house, for example. It's easy to count your outs, but knowing if they're tainted calls for considerable skill.

But let's say you think you'll be able to win two extra $10 bets on the river should you make your flush. You can mentally add that additional $20 to the existing $40-pot, giving you 6-to-1 pot odds. Now your pot odds are better than your drawing odds, so a call here gives you positive expectation—even though many times you'll miss your flush and have to fold the river.

Implied Odds

This notion of counting on future bets if you get lucky and make a big drawing hand is called *implied odds*. While pot odds exist only in relation to the current pot, implied odds exist only with more cards and bets to come.

Just as for flushes, outs and odds can be calculated for drawing to such hands as straights, three-of-a-kind, full houses, and so on. In each case, the comparison is between the cards left in the deck that won't help you versus those that will.

As we said, you won't be working with odds and outs quite yet—the rules of thumb you'll learn will be enough. Just for fun, though, flip to Appendix B and take a look at the odds tables there. Good players are so motivated they learn these by heart—something to bear in mind if you get serious.

Drawing Hands, Made Hands, and Trash Hands

You may have noticed the term *drawing hand* being thrown about in the preceding section. As we said, the archetypal drawing hands are straights and flushes: unless you actually make your straight or flush, you generally fold on the river, since you can't even beat a lowly pair of Deuces.

The opposite of a drawing hand is a *made hand*—a hand that doesn't need to improve to have a chance of being the winner. A pair of Kings in the hole is a good example, since Kings will win many a pot unimproved.

It's true that pocket Kings *can* improve, but this doesn't happen very often. In the outs tables in Appendix B, you'll see that while a flush draw has nine outs and a straight draw has eight outs, two Kings in the hole usually have only their two fellow regents as outs if they hope to improve to three-of-a-kind.

Aside from pocket pairs, another common made hand is top pair. Typically you make this hand when you hold two big cards, for example AQ, and the flop pairs one of them—in this case, coming either Ace-high or Queen-high. Naturally, the bigger your top pair, the better.

What Drawing Hands Want

Lots of other players in the pot, and a cheap initial price. This will give you good pot odds to see the flop and good implied odds if you do flop a draw. After all, most of the time you won't flop even the ghost of a draw, and will have to fold then and there. More on this in the next chapter.

What Made Hands Want

Preferably, to be up against a couple of other weaker made hands or worse. For example, if you flopped a pair of Jacks, you'd be happy to have a player who flopped a pair of Nines as your sole opponent—neither hand has much chance of improving, and unless the Nines improve they'll never beat the Jacks.

What made hands *don't* want is to be surrounded by a lot of drawing hands on a flop that favors the drawing hands. This is one reason why players with two big cards usually raise pre-flop—to cut down the number of draws. Otherwise it's like a bear surrounded by a pack of wolves: the bear may be bigger, but the numbers favor the wolves.

Raise It Up

The biggest exception to made hands not liking company is the single best hand there is—pocket Aces. One of the reasons pocket rockets *are* the best hand is that they win the most money no matter how many players are in the pot. Mingling with the mob or tête-à-tête—Aces are happy either way.

For example, let's say a player raises before the flop with AQ but gets a host of callers. The flop comes with a Queen, giving our hero a pair of Queens. If this player is unlucky enough to be up against a middle straight draw, a smaller pocket pair, and a flush draw, as many as 17 unseen cards in the deck could give someone a better hand than Queens.

This may not sound too bad—except that if everyone sticks around for both the turn and the river, the probability that someone will beat the Queens is roughly 60 percent! This nasty situation (from the made hand's point of view) is called *reverse implied odds*. Keep it in mind as we go forward.

What Trash Hands Want

To be thrown into the muck each time they're dealt to you.

Trash hands are hole cards like 83, J2, and so on. They can't flop a draw, have little chance of flopping a winning top pair, and you will be dealt them more than any other kind of hand. The only rational response is to fold them, but do you know why?

It's not because they're ugly—it's because they have negative expectation. Do the math, and you find they don't make the winning hand often enough to justify paying even a fraction of a bet for them. Ever.

Many losing players love *suited trash*—hands where both hole cards are suited, but far apart in rank, such as J2s or 83s. These players reason that such hands have just as good a chance of flopping a flush draw as suited hands where the cards are close in rank, such as JTs or T8s. The problem is that the *only* way suited trash can win is with a flush, whereas a hand like JTs can also make a straight or in rare cases top pair that holds up.

These extra ways to win give hands like JTs positive expectation when played right—whereas suited trash has negative expectation unless you're in the blinds and can get in cheap. Players who don't know about expectation will keep paying for suited trash over and over, remembering the few big pots they win and forgetting all the chips they dribble away in between.

Delusions of Squander

For fun, let's revisit the list of losing notions we started out with and pinpoint the exact problem with each. Try covering up the answers and thinking first, to see how much you've learned.

Q: Winning most of the pots means winning most of the money, right?

A: This would be true if all pots were the same size—but they're not. A better strategy is to try and make the few pots you're likely to win as big as possible. This is one of the reasons you raise with big pocket pairs like AA and KK before the flop: You have a far better chance of winning than usual, so you're seeking the maximum donation from everyone at the table.

Q: If I play as many hands as possible, doesn't that give me more chances to win?

A: Hold'em isn't a lottery, where every ticket has the same chance of winning; good cards have positive expectation, and bad cards have negative expectation. If you're getting dealt nothing but bad cards, keep folding till your luck changes.

Q: If you see it with your own eyes, it must be true—so what better guide than personal experience to rating your hole cards?

A: That kind of thinking is so short-term you're liable to catch amnesia. Remember, you're in quest of an ideal. You want to play the cards that average a profit over time, not the cards that got lucky yesterday.

The Least You Need to Know

- Mathematical expectation—whether you'll make or lose money in the long run—is the secret behind every decision to check, fold, call, bet, or raise.

- Keep track of your pot odds by comparing the pot size to the size of the current bet; compare this ratio to your chances of winning to determine your best play.

- Experienced players calculate their chances of making a winning flush or straight by counting the cards in the deck that will help them, but beginners can rely on rules of thumb.

- Drawing hands such as straights and flushes want lots of company and no raises before the flop to ensure positive expectation.

- Trash hands are your most common hole cards, but they have such negative expectation that you should nearly always refuse to play them—even if they're suited.

Chapter 4

Getting the Right Price Pre-Flop

In This Chapter

- Luck before the flop versus luck after
- Why position matters
- Hold'em hand groups
- Picking good hands by position
- Pre-flop quiz

It's often been said that the most important decision you make in Hold'em is what hole cards to play, and what to throw away. And we don't disagree. The easiest way to be a consistent loser in Hold'em is to play too many hands before the flop.

The good news is that pre-flop hand selection is also the easiest part of the game to learn. Let's take a look at the hands you will and won't be playing, and why.

Abbreviations for Hole Cards

By their very nature, abbreviations for hole cards help classify pre-flop hands into one type or another. This will give you a jump on learning good pre-flop play, which is all about creating the right circumstances for a given type of hand.

Hole Card Abbreviations

Example	Meaning
AKs, JTs, 98s	The "s" indicates the cards are suited—for example, the Ace and King of Clubs and the Ace and King of Hearts are both written AKs.
AK, T8, 98	Without an "s" these same cards are offsuit, that is, not suited.
Ax, Kx, Qx	The "x" after a face card refers to any card below a Nine. Here, Kx could mean anything from K8 to K2.
Axs, Kxs, Qxs	The same type of hand as above, only suited.

Maneuvering Before the Flop

Hold'em is really two different games: before the flop, and after. The addition of three flop cards all at once has a galvanic effect on the value of your hand. Sometimes it becomes super-charged; more often it gets toasted.

Say you're dealt a powerhouse like AKs, or "Big Slick." You raise and get called by a loosey-goosey player holding J8, a hand whose long-term value is roughly that of snail slime. Lo, the flop comes JJ8, giving snail slime a full house and Big Slick a fast trip to the muck pile.

But don't get the idea that the flop is all that matters, and start playing every hand, waiting until after the flop to decide whether to fold. Hands like AKs flop good far more often than hands like J8—and when AKs and J8 both flop good, AKs will come out on top. You've got to think selectively, or your chips will disappear so fast you'll think someone bored a hole in the table.

Given the uncertainty of the flop and the importance of being frugal, your goal before the flop should be to provide your hand with the circumstances in which it does best. If you think you can't arrange those circumstances, it's often best to fold.

For example, high-card hands that hope to flop top pair should usually raise before the flop to knock out draws. Taking this logic a step further, if enough players are already in that a raise won't narrow the field, you're actually better off folding some of the weaker high-card hands.

Raise It Up

Don't count on getting good hands often. There are 169 possible two-card starting hands you can be dealt in Hold'em—and more than half of them are so weak you should almost never play them. Two unpaired low cards of different suits are among the worst hands. The very best hands feature two high cards, with a pair of Aces the leader of the pack.

The Imposition of Position

Another factor is your position relative to the dealer button. It's so vital, special terms have evolved to describe it. Here, we're talking about a full 10-player game:

- **Under the gun** means the player first to act before the flop. That's the person to the immediate left of the big blind. As the term suggests, he's under considerable pressure.

- **Early position** before the flop refers to the under-the-gun player plus the two players to his left; after the flop, it includes the blinds, since they will now be acting before anyone else if they're still in.

- **Middle position** refers to the next three or four players.
- **Late position** includes the *cutoff*, the player immediately before the button, as well as the button himself.

Talk Like a Texan

The **cutoff** is so named because the player in this seat can try to "cut off" the player on the button by raising before the flop. If the button folds to this ploy, the cutoff inherits his privilege of being last to act on every street after the flop.

Position affects how much information you have, and that affects your ability to safely play certain kinds of hands. For example, in early position you don't know how many players or raises will come after you, so you've got to be cautious and play only very big hands. If you're dealt a potential drawing hand like 55, you've usually got to muck it, for fear of a raise behind you or getting too few callers.

In late position, you know more and have less to fear. If a lot of players have called with no raise, that same 55 becomes eminently playable. And if everyone has folded to you, you can raise with Swiss cheese in an attempt to steal the blinds.

Hold'em Hand Groups

We've arrived at the juicy section of this chapter: the classification of playable hands into different groups.

These hand groups are something of an illusion, like dividing a piano keyboard into octaves: in reality the keyboard is a continuous sequence of notes from top to bottom, but the concept of octaves lets us talk about groups of notes near each other.

Likewise, Hold'em hands are fluid by nature, slipping up and down in value according to the situation. Experience will eventually teach you to judge each hand on its own merits, but the hand groups are a useful crutch when starting out.

Take a moment to scan the chart, then refer back to it as necessary as we discuss each group in turn.

Hold'em Hand Groups

Offsuit Raisers	Suited Raisers
AK, AQ	AKs, AQs
KQ, AJ	KQs, AJs
AT, KJ	ATs, KJs
A9, KT, QJ	A9s, KTs, QJs
Ax, Kx, JT	Ax, Kxs, JTs

Big pairs	Medium pairs	Baby pairs
AA, KK, QQ	TT, 99	66 - 22
JJ	88, 77	

Straight-Flush Draws	Straight-Only Draws	Gapped Straight-Flush Draws
JTs, T9s	JT	QTs, J9s
87s, 76s	T9, 98, 76	T8s, 97s

Notes on the Hand Groups

If you don't see a hand listed in the previous table, chances are it's rarely playable unless you're in the blinds and can see the flop for free or for a fraction of a bet.

Within each group, hands are listed in order of strength. For example, you can play the top Offsuit Raiser, AK, in any position. But the hands on the last rung in this group—Ax, Kx, and JT—are almost unplayable as raising hands unless you're the small blind trying to steal from the big blind. This is largely due to fear of *domination*.

Talk Like a Texan

Domination occurs when a raiser's hand is so much better than your hand that you almost can't beat him—even though yours is a raising hand, too. Two examples are AK and AQ. If an Ace comes on the flop, the AQ will find it hard to fold, even though it's doomed by its second-best kicker. To avoid domination, tend not to call raises unless you hold a hand near the top end of the raiser's likely range of hands given his position.

Other hand groups are less variable: For example, hands belonging to the Baby Pairs and the various Draws can be played similarly, despite differences in relative strength. Exploring such differences can wait until you gain experience.

Playable Hands by Position

Position is the single most critical factor before the flop. So the easiest way to start learning the hand groups is by changing seats around the table, seeing in each case what we can play.

As before, we'll assume a full table with 10 players. Often that won't be the case, but adjusting for fewer players is easy. Say for example that there are only seven players. The under-the-gun player is now in the same exact seat as a middle-position player would be if the game were full—so he should play his hands the same way as if he were in middle position in a full game, and everyone ahead of him had folded.

Or say there are just five players. In that case, the player under the gun is in the same seat as the cutoff in a full game. He should play his hands exactly as if he *were* the cutoff in a full game and, once again, everyone ahead of him had folded.

Early Position: Tight Is Right

As we've stated, if you're in the first few seats before the flop, you lack the information to safely play anything but your very best hands. At all but the most *passive* tables, you're forced to fold drawing hands for fear of a raise behind you. Likewise you play only your top raising hands, for fear of domination.

Talk Like a Texan

Passive is at the opposite end of **aggressive** in poker. Passive players rarely raise before the flop without an absolute monster, while aggressive players raise whenever a good opportunity comes along. You'll learn more about this and other ways of categorizing your opponents in the chapters to come.

Early, and No One Has Raised

Go ahead and raise with all your big pairs, and in a *tight* game—a game where few players tend to call before the flop—raise as well with the two biggest medium pairs, TT and 99. With QQ, KK, and AA you don't care how many people call, but with 99, TT, and even JJ, you're hoping to get just one or two callers to boost the chances your pair will be best hand on the flop.

Also raise with the top rungs in the Offsuit Raisers and Suited Raisers—AK, AQ, AKs, and AQs. If you're adventurous, you can raise with KQs and AJs as well, but be aware these latter hands are more easily dominated. The only reason you can raise with them is because they're suited, giving you an extra way to win.

> **Raise It Up** _____
>
> Here's a trick often used by experienced players: Once in a while, **limp** AA and KK instead of raising—that is, just call with them, as if you had an ordinary or even a weak hand. What you're hoping for is you'll get some limpers and then a raise, allowing you to put in a second raise. The pot will be huge by the time you get to the flop, and you'll have an enormous head start.

Fold all other hands in this position for now. Certain types of games let you play drawing hands up front, but you can only judge this once you've gained considerable experience.

Early, and Someone Has Raised

If the under-the-gun player raises and you're next in line, now you truly must play tight: Until evidence shows otherwise, assume the raiser has at least as good a hand as you'd have in his spot. If no one else calls, you'll be head-up with the raiser, so whatever you're holding had better be good.

With QQ, KK, AA, and possibly JJ, your best play is not to call but to reraise. These hands are good enough that there's a chance you're better than the raiser if he's holding a smaller pair or a hand like AQ or AK. With AKs you can call or reraise, depending on whether you want to try and lure other players in so you'll win a big pot should you make a flush. For similar reasons, you can chance calling with AQs—but only if the table is playing loose enough that you'll get company.

Middle Position: A Little Looser

Sitting in the middle of the lineup, the possibilities expand, and your hand selection can expand a little more, too.

Middle, and No One Has Opened

When you *open the pot*, you become the first player to voluntarily put chips into the pot, by either calling or raising the big blind. So either you're first to act, or else everyone before you has folded.

When opening in middle position, it's usually best to raise, for the same reasons as you would under the gun. But now you can raise with hands as weak as KQ and AJ, as well as those already mentioned. And you're definitely raising with TT and 99.

Middle, and Several Players Have Called

The presence of two to four callers in the pot ahead of you means you must tighten up a little with raises, but can loosen up with your better drawing hands.

You can still raise with your powerhouses: AK, AQ, AKs, AQs, all the big pairs, and even KQs and AJs. But you need to think about whether to raise with a hand slightly weaker than these such as KQ and AJ. Many good players do, but only if they feel they're up against weak opposition. When you're just starting out, it's fine to call with hands such as these and hope for a good flop.

You can limp drawing hands on the order of JTs, T9s, 88, 77, and in a passive game QTs and J9s. You're hoping no one will raise behind you.

Middle, and There's a Raise with No Callers Yet

This depends on where the raise came from. If it's from under the gun, you must still fold all but your very best hands.

But if the raise came from the middle player just in front of you, now you can call or possibly reraise with even the weakest of your early-position raising hands. The raiser could still have a powerhouse, but given his position, it's less likely. For example, you'd probably reraise with AQ.

Middle, and There's a Raise with Several Callers

You can play all the quality hands we mentioned before, but now you can consider cautiously adding JTs, TT, and 99. But you must be careful: if you don't get a great flop, you'll have to fold them. If you do hit a great flop you stand to win a bigger pot than usual.

With JTs, you're hoping for a straight or flush draw; with TT and 99, you're looking to flop either a set or top pair. Top pair isn't very likely, and neither is a set, but the two possibilities combined are just enough.

Late Position: Time to Limp or Else Get Aggressive

By now you have lots of information and much less concern about what someone will do in back of you—only the blinds remain. But you still must play the right hands for the situation.

Late, and No One Has Opened

Here's where the weaker members of the Offsuit and Suited Raisers come into their own. As cutoff or even a seat before, you can open-raise with AT and KJ, plus their suited variants. As dealer, you can open-raise with A9, KT, and QJs.

With so few players left, there's a good chance your relatively weak raising hand is in fact the best hand. Your goal here is to steal the blinds or get head-up with one other weaker hand—but be aware that if you're playing in a casino at a very low limit table, the rake may be so brutal that a purely steal hand should be folded. See Chapter 9 for exactly why.

Late, and Many Players Have Called

If lots of players are in and no one has raised, you'll be able to limp your full range of drawing hands, including all the Straight-Flush Draws and Gapped Straight-Flush Draws. Most of the time, you'll have to fold when the flop misses your hand. But when you *do* hit, having this many players in means you'll have a shot at winning an extra-large pot.

Late, and There's a Raise with No Callers Yet

Position counts here. If the raise came from an early position, you must play tight as before. But if, for example, the cutoff raises, you can chance a reraise with as little as AT, A9s, and 66. Your goal is to get head-up and hope he was trying to steal.

If you've got a monster like AA, you might want to just call a late raise to disguise the nature of your hand, but this is a riskier option, one you'll have to gain experience with.

Late, and There's a Raise with Many Callers

This isn't too dissimilar from a middle raise with several callers: JTs and the medium pairs are playable with five or more players in the pot ahead of you. And if it's a *family pot*, with the whole table calling so far, you can call with the baby pairs and the smaller Straight-Flush draws. The pot will be so big that the extra price you're paying to draw is just worth it.

The only thing to be careful about is a game where players love to gamble and raising is epidemic: It's one thing to pay two bets for the privilege of draw-ing with a hand like 87s, but if the action moves back around and an early limper puts in a reraise just for fun, it hurts your expectation. Therefore, consider the likelihood of a reraise before calling with your weaker hands.

The Blinds: Free Looks and Bargains

When you're in the small blind, you'll already have part of a bet in the pot. In the big blind, you'll have a whole bet invested. This causes many players to automatically complete the bet in the small blind or call raises in the big blind. But you shouldn't do anything automatically. Instead, consider the following strategies for different situations.

Watch Your Chips

Beware of calling too many raises when you're in the blinds, especially the small blind. Sure, you're getting a discount, but that doesn't mean that paying a bet and a half or a bet and two thirds for total trash suddenly becomes a great deal. If you were in the market for a good used car, would you buy a wreck with no tires or motor, just because it was cheap?

In the Blinds, and No Raise

In the small blind, go ahead and call with any hand in any of the hand groups. With many players in, you can even call with suited trash, a hand you'd normally fold. The discount you're getting plus your good pot odds have made the difference.

In either the small or big blind, with hands as good as KK, AA, AQs, AKs, and AK, prefer to raise to build the pot. You're so much better than the average starting hand that you want more money in for those times you flop a monster. If only a few players are in, you can also raise with QQ. If it's just the dealer limping in, go ahead and raise with any of the hands you'd raise with in early position.

In the Blinds, and a Raise

If four or more players have already called the raise, or look like they'll call when the action gets back to them, you can call in the small blind with your better drawing hands and the hands you'd raise with in early position. And you should put in a second raise yourself with KK, AA, AKs, and AQs. The big blind can raise with these hands as well, and can also call with any drawing hand, not just the better draws.

If no one has called the raiser yet, or if there's just one or two callers, you must tighten up considerably. JTs might be the weakest of the drawing hands you'd call with in the small blind.

Again, consider the raiser's position: If he raised under the gun and you're contemplating being the sole caller in either of the blinds, you'll need a powerful hand. The big blind can play a trifle looser than the small blind—but stay away from dominated hands.

For example, if the raise is from under the gun and you're in the big blind with AT, you're better off folding even though your hand is fairly respectable. There's too much chance you'll flop an Ace, call all the way, and get shown AQ, AK, or AJs. You'd actually be better off calling with a hand like 98s or 88 that seeks to exploit flops with small cards.

Quiz on Pre-Flop Play

Let's see how much you've learned. Again, we'll assume a full game with all 10 seats filled.

Q: The under-the-gun player limps in, and you're next. What do you do with AJ? 76s? TT?

A: *AJ:* Fold. If both the limper and you were in middle position, you could raise, but you're not. *76s:* Also fold—you don't know whether enough players will come in without a raise behind you. *TT:* In a loose game, call in hopes of luring players in behind you and flopping a set; in a tight game, raise to narrow the field. Your medium-big pair plays well either way.

Q: Everyone folds to a middle position player, who open-raises. He gets one caller before the action comes to you on the button. What do you do with JJ? 76s? AQ?

A: *JJ:* Reraise, in hopes of knocking out the blinds. Your big pair will play much better, with less fear of overcards, if you can narrow the field. *76s:* Fold. This smallish drawing hand requires a family pot or position in the blinds before it can call a raise. *AQ:* It's a toss-up between calling and raising. Like JJ, this hand would do better if you could narrow the field, but unlike JJ, you don't have a made hand yet. If the raiser is a tough player, calling is best.

Q: You're in the small blind, with four limpers to you and no raise yet. Just half a bet, and you're in—but of course you can raise, too. What do you do with 44? QQ? 96?

A: *44:* Call. This is a good drawing hand with many callers and the discount. *QQ:* Another tough decision. You probably have best hand before the flop, but your position will be the worst possible thereafter, and for a big pair Queens are surprisingly vulnerable. Probably it's best to just call here and reserve any fireworks for the flop. *96:* Fold. Yes, you are getting a discount and your pot odds look good—but your expectation is still negative.

The Least You Need to Know

- Be selective in choosing which hole cards to play, based on your position relative to the dealer, whether anyone has raised yet, and how many players have already called.

- The earlier your position, the less you know and the more you have to fear, so the stronger your hands must be.

- The later your position, the more you know and the less you have to fear, allowing you to play more draws and raise with weaker hands.

- Hand groups are a convenient way to remember the value of different hole cards, as well as the conditions they favor.

- The blinds give you a discount, allowing you to play more hands—but you've still got to be selective.

Chapter 5

Garbage to Gold (and Vice Versa)

In This Chapter

- Fitting the flop
- Tough choices on the turn
- Maximizing the river
- Post-flop quiz

So you did your best to pick good starting cards—but now the *flop* has come, and you and your opponents are staring at three new cards face-up in the middle of the table. Depending on the nature of your hole cards, these three new cards may make you want to jump out of your chair—or slide under it.

No matter how strong your hole cards—even those mythic pocket Aces—you'll usually be looking for help on the flop. Of course, so will your opponents. The challenge now becomes calculating not just the objective value of your hand by itself, but how it stacks up against the possible hands your opponents may hold.

And there's still the *turn* and *river* to come! With each fresh community card, you must assess and reassess. Do I have the best hand now? Am I drawing to make the best hand? Which cards can help me? Which cards can hurt me? And what are the other players holding, given the *board* and the betting?

It's a tall order. But in this chapter, you' learn how to size up these dicey situations and choose your best play.

Talk Like a Texan

Remember, the **board** refers to the five common cards shared by all the players. The **flop** refers to the first three board cards. The **turn** is the fourth card. And the **river** is the fifth card. It completes the board and gives all players seven cards to work with in making their best poker hand.

Be Flexible on the Flop

The first rule is forget about how pretty or ugly your hole cards looked pre-flop. Whether you were jamming with pocket Kings or limping a dog of a drawing hand, it's chips under the bridge. How your cards mesh or don't mesh with the flop is all that matters now.

With five cards on the board and only two more to go, you're seeing 71 percent of the cards you'll ever see. This is your chance to reevaluate the present and future value of your hand.

At the same time, you also have to factor in the betting, your position at the table, the size of the pot, and the odds your hand will improve by catching a helping card on the turn.

Raise It Up

A weak hand in a big pot can be worth more than a strong hand in a small one. For example, let's say you have a 20 percent chance (1 in 5) of winning a $100 pot. In that situation, your hand is "worth" $20. Now what if you have a better hand—say one with a 50 percent chance of winning— but the pot is just $30? This hand is worth just $15.

This method of valuing a hand is known as **pot equity**. In small pots, you may find your pot equity won't justify calling even a single bet, while in big pots even a relatively slim chance of winning can make it well worth your while to play on.

In calculating this last factor, there's an added consideration: might a card that helps you help an opponent even more? For example, if you hold 89 and the flop comes TJ3, a Queen on the turn can make you a straight—but it would also make a higher straight for anyone holding K9 or AK.

To help you get a feel for playing the flop, we analyze some common situations in the next few pages. We also included a table, "Matching Your Hole Cards to the Flop," that lays out some specific situations.

Made Hands on the Flop

Sometimes you'll have a hand that's likely to be the best on the flop. Say you started with KQ and the flop comes QT7. You've "flopped good," making top pair (Queens) with the second highest possible kicker (the King).

You'll usually want to play this hand aggressively, by putting in a bet or raise. There's a good chance you're winning, so you want to get as many bets here as you can from the other players.

Furthermore, with this flop, someone could be drawing to a straight with a hand like 89. Most of the time they'll miss their draw on the turn and river, and in the meantime you certainly don't want to let them draw for free when they could be paying you for the privilege.

Drawing Hands on the Flop

Other times you'll be the one drawing. For example, if you limped in with A♥6♥ and the flop came K♥9♥2♠, you'd have a draw to the best possible flush.

You'll usually want to play a drawing hand more passively than a made hand. In this example, anyone with a pair is ahead of you right now. If there's a bet to you, you'll often just call. If you raise, you'll not only be putting money in with a hand that could end up being nearly worthless, you may also make other players fold. You don't really want that to happen—you want them around to call your bets if you make your flush.

Sometimes, though, you *will* want to bet or raise with a draw. The odds of making your flush by the river are about 2 to 1 against. So if three or more players are in the pot, you're actually getting positive odds if they all call. What's more, a bet or raise on the flop might make opponents check to you on the turn. Then, if the turn card doesn't make your flush, you can check along and see the river card for free.

Matching Your Hole Cards to the Flop

Hole Cards	Flop
AA	**K82 of different suits**

What you like: This is a very good flop for you. Your top pair is likely to be the best hand and there are no flush or straight possibilities.

What to watch for: All you really have to fear is someone with pocket Kings, Eights, or Deuces who would now have three of a kind, or maybe a hand like K8s that has flopped two pair. Bet if checked to and raise if someone else bets.

55	**5AQ with two cards of the same suit**

What you like: Prepare to win some chips. You've got a *set* of Fives and a player with an Ace or a Queen is likely to give you action.

What to watch for: If someone calls all bets on this two-suited flop, or even tosses in a raise, they could have a flush draw. If a third suited card hits on the turn, and that player starts betting and raising, he may have made his flush. The good news is that if the board pairs on the river, you'll make a full house and beat him.

AKs	**678 all of one suit, different from yours**

What you like: Not much. Your powerful starting hand has completely missed this flop. If you have only one opponent, you may have the best hand—for now.

What to watch for: You could already be losing badly to a made flush or straight. Pairing an Ace or King on the turn won't be enough to beat either of these hands. If there's a bet and call in front of you, it could be folding time.

Hole Cards	Flop
JTs	6QK with one card of your suit

What you like: You have an *open-ended draw* (meaning that you can make a straight with either a Nine or an Ace) to the best possible straight, plus a *backdoor* flush draw if the turn and river cards are both your suit.

What to watch for: Anyone with a King or Queen is beating you right now. You have eight outs (four Nines and four Aces) to give you the highest possible straight, so you won't fold. But for now you'll usually want to be a caller, not a bettor.

Talk Like a Texan

From Chapter 2, you'll remember that a **set** is three-of-a-kind made by holding a pocket pair when a third card of that rank is on the board. You can also make three-of-a-kind by matching one of your hole cards with two paired cards on the board. That hand is called **trips**.

Position on the Flop and Beyond

Your position relative to the other players is at least as important on the flop, turn, and river as it was pre-flop. Whenever you're the first to bet or check, everyone else has an advantage over you. They can fold their weak hands, or bet or raise with their strong ones. Plus if you check, they can use their position to bet a weak hand, in hopes you'll fold.

When you're last to act, *you* have the same advantage. You no longer have to guess what the other players might do, and this lets you play more aggressively. For example, say you limped in behind four other players with A5s on the button. If the flop comes A93 of different suits and everyone checks, you can bet with a fair amount of confidence that your pair of Aces is best, despite your rag kicker.

One way to turn all this around and make early position an advantage with certain hands is by using the *check-raise*. Say you've flopped a moderately good hand like top pair. You'd like to protect it by knocking out as many opponents as possible. But you're in early position—if you bet here, you could easily get several callers. What to do?

Try this: Check meekly, as if the flop missed you. Hopefully everyone else will check to a late-position player. If he bets, you'll now have the chance to raise and confront the other players with the prospect of calling not just one bet, but two. If they don't hold strong hands, they may well fold where they would have called a single bet.

Of course if everyone checks, you can't raise. So it's best to use this maneuver when you think someone *will* bet. Also, the exact effect depends on the position of the bettor. For example, let's say you're first to act and there are four players behind you. If you check and the next player bets, the other players will have either folded already or else called the

single bet before the action gets back to you. In
that situation, a check raise isn't likely to knock
anyone out.

Raise It Up

Back in Chapter 2, we emphasized the
need to always know the nuts—that is,
the best hand that someone can hold with
whatever common cards are showing. Just
remember that most times, no one will
actually *have* the nuts. If you've got a
hand like a pair of Nines and the flop
comes AA7, often no one has an Ace.
There are only two Aces left in the deck,
so you very well may have the best
hand—even though it's not the best *possible* hand.

To the Turn

With a fourth card on the board, your hand has
either improved or it hasn't. If it hasn't, there's now
only one more chance for help instead of two.

Another crucial factor is that in most limit games,
the bet size doubles on the turn. For example, in a
$2-4 game, the maximum bet is $2 before the flop
and on the flop, but $4 on the turn and river.

All this means that while the flop may be easy street, the turn is the tough side of town. Many low-limit players will call the flop with almost anything, but a call on the turn often betrays either a real hand or a real draw.

Moreover, the increased bet size induces seemingly paradoxical behavior on the part of players who flop extremely powerful hands such as trips, sets, straights, or flushes. You might expect them to play the flop aggressively, but in fact many prefer to check and call as meekly as your Aunt Edna.

Why? First, a player with a monster doesn't want to drive off her customers—she'd rather have as many players as possible stick around. Second, by just calling any flop bets, she hopes to lull the bettor into betting the turn as well. Now when she raises, she'll earn twice as much with the double-size bet.

Whether you're looking at the nuts or nada, the turn calls for some planning on your part. Because there's only one card to go, you now have to consider not just how you'll play your hand here, but how to play the river as well. Let's look at some typical scenarios.

Made Hands on the Turn

If you think you're ahead, you'll want to get your money in now. Often the pot has gotten pretty big and you won't mind if everyone folds to your turn bet and you win right here.

Sometimes the turn will complete a draw for you. In the best case, you'll hold not just the nuts, but also the pure nuts: no matter what card comes on the river, it can't make a hand that will beat yours. An example of this would be when you've flopped a four flush with 10♥9♥ on a board like Q♥8♥ 4♣ and the turn makes you a straight flush with the J♥. Your only problem is figuring out how to milk the maximum number of bets from the other players!

Unfortunately, most hands aren't this strong. Often you'll have a good hand, such as top pair, that may still be the best on the turn, but continues to be pursued by several opponents. They're hoping for a good river card, but most of the time they won't get it.

Bet or raise strongly to lower their odds and charge them the maximum for their draw, just as you would on the flop. In any one hand, they may draw out on you, but you can't let this make you timid.

Sometimes the turn card makes a straight or flush possible right then and there. If a normally passive opponent starts raising the moon at this point and you hold only a fair hand such as top pair, you'll probably want to fold—you can't possibly improve to beat the hand they're representing. But if the raiser is tricky or over-aggressive, you may be better off calling, especially if the pot is large. Likewise, if you hold a set, you have a *redraw*, meaning your hand can still improve on the river to beat a straight or flush. In that case, a call is again in order.

Drawing Hands on the Turn

Because of the sudden jump on the turn to a double-size bet, you must be extra-careful of your drawing odds versus your pot odds. For example, you might be able to call a single bet and still have positive expectation, but not a bet and a raise. Smart opponents who've put you on a draw will often raise the turn solely for the purpose of hurting your odds or knocking you out, whether or not their own hand is strong.

In calculating your odds, think carefully about how many outs you *really* have to improve to a winning hand. It can be quite expensive when your hand improves on the river, but not enough to win.

For example, say you're holding A♠K♠ and the board on the turn is J♠8♠3♥9♦. It's tempting to think that in addition to your nine flush outs, you've got an extra four outs by counting the remaining Aces and Kings not of your suit. But would making top pair on the river be enough to win? If you have only one opponent, there's a good chance it would.

However, let's say it's a four-way pot and the cut-off's eyes lit up at the sight of the Nine. If he now starts raising like he's turned the straight, you'll probably have to beat that hand to win. That puts you back at your nine flush outs, not the 13 combined outs you were hoping for.

Betting the Turn

It can be correct to bet the turn even when you don't have a made hand or a draw, especially when you have one opponent who may also be weak.

Let's say you raised pre-flop with AK and got two callers. The flop came T73 of different suits, you bet out again, and one player folded. Now the turn brings a Four. If your sole remaining opponent has so much as a pair of Deuces, he's ahead. Nevertheless, it's often correct to bet your hand again.

Why? First, the larger bet size and your persistent aggression may convince your opponent to fold a better hand than yours, such as the Deuces we just mentioned. Second, if he's on a draw, your Ace-high may beat him if he doesn't make that draw. By betting, you're making him call a bet at even odds in a situation where you're actually the favorite. That's always a +EV situation for you. (That's shorthand for positive expectation.)

Getting Raised on the Turn

What happens when you bet the turn and someone raises? As in our previous example, say you raise with AK before the flop. The flop comes K43, giving you top pair. You of course bet. When the turn brings an innocuous-seeming Deuce, you bet again, but get raised! There are a couple of possibilities to consider here.

If the raiser is a fairly passive, straightforward player, there's a good chance he flopped something strong, like a set of Fours or Threes, and was merely waiting for the double-size betting round to pound you.

If he's a loose player, another possibility is that he called your pre-flop raise with something puny like 65, a hand good players would routinely throw away versus a raise. If so, the Four just gave him his straight. You've shown strength throughout the hand, so it's unlikely he's bluffing.

Given how we've categorized your opponent, a fold could be in order in such cases. But let's say you're head-up against a loose, tricky opponent who could raise with a wide range of hands here, including many that your top pair, top kicker can beat. In that case you have an easy call and could even ponder reraising.

Folding the Turn

Even when you *aren't* raised, sometimes it's correct to call the flop, but fold the turn. Say you're dealt QJs in middle position in a $2-$4 game. You limp in and someone raises behind you. You and two others call and the flop comes AK3. It's checked to the pre-flop raiser and she bets. One person calls, one folds, and now it's up to you.

As it happens, you can call a single flop bet on the chance the turn will bring a Ten, giving you the nut straight. Let's do the math: Eight $2 bets went into the pot before the flop (two bets from each of four players) and now two more have gone in on the flop. So you're getting 10-to-1 odds to call the $2. The four Tens you hope are in the deck give you four outs, making your odds of hitting a straight on the next card roughly 11 to 1 against it happening. Assuming a straight will indeed be a winner, and that you'll win some additional bets if you make it, calling here is positive expectation.

Now the turn card comes a Five. The same player bets, the other player in the hand folds, and it's up to you. This time, you'll probably have to fold. True, the pot is now bigger at $26 (the $22 in previous bets plus your opponent's $4 turn bet), but the double-size bet means you're getting less than 7 to 1 pot odds. The chances of making your straight haven't improved—you're still looking at roughly 11 to 1 against. The result? Your expectation for calling has abruptly flipped from positive to negative.

While we're on the subject of odds, take a moment to glance at the odds tables in Appendix B. Get familiar with these—it'll make your turn calculations a lot easier.

On the River

Every hand is a completed hand once the fifth and final card hits the board. You know for sure what you have, but that doesn't mean playing the river is easy. You'll often face tough decisions about whether to bet, call, raise, or fold. How well you make them will have a major effect on your winnings.

Betting the River

The most important time to bet the river is when you're probably ahead. Say you have AK, there's an Ace on the board and no likely draw. Two opponents have been calling your bets and now you wonder if you should bet your top pair, top kicker one more time. Often, you should. Players with an Ace and a worse kicker are likely to call. Even someone with a lower pair may call "just to keep you honest."

Such bets are based on the value of your hand. It may feel easier to check the river, especially since you win either way—but by failing to bet, you're failing to capture profit that should be yours. Over time, these lost bets add up.

The more opponents you have, the stronger your hand should be to bet for value. If three people have stayed to the river, one of them is likely to have top pair beaten. And if your value bet gets raised, seriously consider folding. A bluff is always theoretically possible—but bluff-raising the river doesn't happen often.

Build Your Stack

Unlike the grim silence of a serious chess match, coffeehousing is a time-honored poker tradition. When a third suited card hits on the turn, your opponent might declare "I've got the flush now," while you respond, "So do I—how high is yours?" Even if neither of you really has a flush, it's considered okay by most players to misrepresent your hand. Rules and conventions regarding table talk vary from player to player and from place to place. When in doubt, we suggest erring on the side of discretion.

Folding the River

When you miss a draw to a flush or straight, you'll often have a hand that's nearly worthless and an easy fold. Likewise, when you have a so-so hand and someone bets, be inclined to fold if there are other players still to act behind you. A weaker hand is much less likely to bet, either for value or as a bluff, with many potential callers.

It's harder to fold when you have a reasonably good hand, like two pair. But you may be wise to do so if there's a bet and a raise to you and the board makes possible a straight, flush, or full house.

Calling the River

Remember we told you to be sure and bet the river for value? Well, that's often true. But some hands are good candidates for checking the river and calling if your opponent bets.

There are a couple of reasons for this. First, if you're not sure about the value of your hand, it may be worth a call but not a bet, for fear of a raise. Second, by checking in early position, you may induce a player to bluff-bet a weaker hand. That alone can add to your profits significantly over time.

Then there's the special case of being head-up against an opponent whom you feel may have been on a draw. You won't always know by the board whether he made it or not. If he missed, he'll fold, so you won't gain anything by betting. But if he made his draw, he'll probably raise. Either way, you're better off checking and just calling if he bets.

Finally, there are times when the pot gets huge on early rounds and everyone but you and one or two other players fold by the river. Be inclined to call with even a slim chance of winning when the pot is big. After all, if there are 10 bets in the pot, you only have to win one time in nine to make a call +EV.

Raising the River

The time to raise the river is almost always when you're confident of victory. That's because most opponents won't fold for one more bet, even though your raise signals to them that they're probably beat.

It's easy to raise the river when you have the nuts, or very close to it. As you improve, you'll be able to see opportunities to raise with lesser hands that are still likely winners.

Quiz on Post-Flop Play

Let's finish up by testing your skills on each betting round:

Q: You raised to open the betting in early position before the flop with A♥Q♥. Two middle-position players called, as did the big blind. The flop comes J♣8♥4♦, and although you were the fearsome pre-flop raiser, the big blind bets out. How do you respond?

A: We've started you off with a tough one! Good arguments can be made for calling, raising, or even folding.

Let's start with calling: Both your cards are higher than the Jack on the board, so if your opponent only has a pair of Jacks, you'd be justified in trying to catch an Ace or Queen on the turn. Your odds of doing so are 6.8 to 1, which compares favorably to your 9-to-1 pot odds.

But what about raising? This might knock out the two players behind you, and get the big blind to check the turn so that you can see the river for free if you don't hit.

Folding becomes your best option if you're worried about a raise from one of the players behind you—especially if you fear someone has flopped a huge hand, something much better than a mere pair of Jacks.

Just to let you know, though, calling here is probably the right play most of the time, given that you have three opponents a relatively unthreatening flop and a bet from the first player to act. So if you gave that as your answer, consider it a more than passing grade.

Q: You raise pre-flop in last position with two black Aces; the four limpers ahead of you call the extra bet. The flop comes 456, with two Hearts. All check, you bet, and two players call. Now the turn adds the T♥, putting a potential flush on board. The player in first position—a quiet type—checks. The player behind her checks, too, so once more you bet. Suddenly, the quiet type springs to life with a check-raise!

A: Kiss your hand and this big pot goodbye, and fold. A passive, quiet player isn't check-raising you and the other player here without the flush. Note that if she does have the flush, there is no card you can get on the river to improve to a winner. Your only reason to call would be if you held the Ace of Hearts, giving you a draw to the nut flush—but you don't.

Q: You're on the river in a smallish pot. You hold QJs and the board is 2JT6K with no flush possible. Two other players are also in, and have passively called your bets on the flop and turn. Now what?

A: Go ahead and bet your pair of Jacks, Queen kicker. Sure, someone might have hit a King on the river, but it's more likely this card didn't change a thing. Anyone with a Ten will likely call you; even a hand like A6 may call. If your bet is raised by anyone who isn't a wild bluffer, you can fold in peace.

The Least You Need to Know

- How well your two hole cards "fit the flop" is a major factor in determining whether to continue—and if you *do* continue, how best to play your hand.

- Being last to act, or nearly so, is at least as big an advantage on the flop as it was pre-flop, and for the same reason: You get to see what your opponents do before they see what you do.

- On the turn, you need a strong hand or draw to continue playing, especially since in most limit games the bet doubles here.

- On the river, concentrate on capturing profit by betting or raising strong hands, cutting losses by folding weak hands, and maximizing the middle ground by checking and calling with fair hands.

Chapter 6

How to Lose—and How to Win

In This Chapter

- Fixing simple mistakes with good habits
- Adjusting to the occasion
- Healing your inner poker player

Remember "Goldilocks and the Three Bears"? Well, there's more similarity than you might imagine between Goldilocks's various dilemmas and yours as you learn to play Hold'em.

Take bluffing, for example: Too much can lose chips in a hurry, but too little can also cost you chips—your smarter opponents learn to quietly fold whenever you've got a big hand. Learning what's "just right" requires a lot of study and a lot of time at the tables.

Generally, we learn in poker by making mistakes and then thinking them over afterward. This chapter speeds up that process with tips to help you improve your judgment and waste less time on common beginner's mistakes.

Many of these mistakes have not only a tactical or strategic component, but an emotional component as well. In such cases, it may not be enough to think in terms of mere avoidance—you need to choose an active counter-strategy. This is especially true for mistakes that are primarily emotional, and are thus the most potentially catastrophic of all to your earnings and enjoyment.

Building Good Habits

Throughout this book, we stress thinking about your responses rather than reacting automatically. However, certain things occur so often, and the speed of play is so quick, that your responses become habitual. An example is looking at your hole cards, seeing that they are trash, and flicking them into the muck.

While this particular habit is usually fine, it's easy to form bad habits in other areas without realizing it. Replacing these with good habits takes conscious practice, but anytime you can plug a *leak* by doing so, it's well worth it.

Talk Like a Texan

In poker, a **leak** is just what it sounds like: a bad habit or mistaken belief that's costing you chips. A good player has as few leaks as possible: she's constantly searching for ways to improve, even when she's winning. A bad player can be as full of leaks as a shower nozzle, but remain completely unaware of it. Instead, he'll blame the cards, the dealers, or the alignment of the planets—anything but his own lack of knowledge or self-control.

Calling Too Many Raises Before the Flop

This is an easy mistake to make—especially when you've been dutiful about throwing away trash hands and haven't seen decent-looking hole cards in a long while.

So what if the under-the-gun player just raised, and everyone has folded to you? You're in middle position holding Q♥J♥, and gosh, those Hearts sure look pretty! You could flop a flush draw, or a straight draw, or a full house …

This is the wrong way to think and the wrong habit to build. Over time, calling pre-flop raises in situations where you don't have expected value leads to exactly what you'd expect—lost chips. So instead of reacting with wishful thinking, take an extra second or two to run through your mental checklist of how to play given categories of hands.

In the example as given, you may wind up head-up with the raiser with a dominated hand. If a Queen or Jack flops, you'll be tempted to call all the way—and those times the raiser shows you the same hand on the river, but with a better kicker, will really hurt. If you were on the button with four other players having called the raiser, a call would be justified—you'd be looking to flop a draw to a big straight or flush in a huge pot.

 Watch Your Chips

> A good rule of thumb is not to call a raise before the flop with any hand you weren't thinking of raising with yourself. In the example in the text, you wouldn't have raised in middle position with Q♥J♥, so you shouldn't be calling a raise with it either. In fact, if no one else has called yet, you often need a stronger hand to *call* a raise than to raise in the first place!

Ignoring or Forgetting About Pot Size

This, too, is easy to do. If you're playing correctly, most of the time you're folding bad hole cards and watching others play out the hand. Who needs to keep track of the pot? You're too busy twiddling your thumbs.

But then you not only pick up a playable drawing hand, you flop an actual draw to go with it. There's a bet across the table, and you've got your chips all ready in your hand to call, when the next player in line raises! Quick—what are your pot odds? Can you call the raise or not? You don't have time to count the jumbled pile of chips, so you hastily call or fold, unsure in either case of whether you did the right thing.

Avoid this scenario by drilling yourself repetitively: any time you're not in the pot, count those chips as the players put forward their individual bets or raises, until it's a habit you can count on.

As a side note, another advantage to not looking at your hole cards until it's your turn to act is that you can pick up *tells*, while avoiding giving any tells yourself. See Chapter 7 for more on this subject.

Raise It Up

Don't try to count the pot by counting the actual dollars—not only is this hard to do, but when it comes time to figure your pot odds, you'll have to expend extra effort dividing the pot size in dollars by the bet size in dollars. For limit poker, it's a lot easier to count the pot by how many bets go in it. This also makes your pot odds easier to figure, because you're always dividing by bets, not dollar amounts.

Adjusting to Fit Your Opponents

Hold'em doesn't reward a one-size-fits-all strategy. One type of opponent may doggedly see the river with 90 percent of his cards, rarely if ever raising; another may raise frequently but fold even more frequently when raised back. If you play these two types the same way, you lose.

You'll learn more about this notion of varying your play in the next chapter. For now, the following sections outline two basic categories of mistakes that can be corrected by equally basic adjustments.

Bluffing Too Much, or Not at All

We've already said that in low-limit Hold'em, most of your opponents err by calling too much. This type of player is a *calling station*—someone you can count on for a lot of profit whenever you have a strong hand and he's got a weak one.

However, if you insist on bluffing calling stations, the advantage shifts to them: In effect they are now using the correct strategy by calling your poorly considered bluffs.

Another beginner's mistake is to bluff in multi-way pots, especially on the river. If it's hard to bluff one typical low-limit player, imagine how hard it is to bluff three or four!

But what if you never bluff, meaning that you only bet or raise with your good hands? In a typical low limit game, that's not nearly as costly a mistake as bluffing too much. Still, as we've already noted, decent players will pick up on this and stop calling whenever you start betting—unless they themselves hold an extremely strong hand, one that could likely beat you.

The cure isn't to start bluffing with any old hand, but to learn an advanced technique called *semi-bluffing*. This involves bluffing with a bet or raise when you don't yet have a hand, but have at least some chance of making a good hand on the next card. We'll explain this technique in Chapter 7, so stick around.

Keeping Everyone Honest—or Folding at the Drop of a Hat

Both of these are unrewarding extremes. As an example of the first, if you find yourself in the habit of glumly calling along when you have a fair hand, while knowing in your heart you're beaten, you may have morphed into a calling station.

It's a matter of judgment, because folding a hand that could have scooped an entire pot is a far greater error than losing an extra bet or two. But if you consistently find yourself staring at better hands at the showdown, you've acquired a leak that you need to correct.

Start by getting rid of the notion that you have to call to "keep players honest." The idea behind this adage is that it's a sin to let anyone win a pot by bluffing. The problem is, this doesn't take into account whom you're calling.

If that fellow who calls along to the river with 90 percent of his hands suddenly starts betting, the chances are excellent he's not bluffing. Even with players you know to be habitual bluffers, you're better off calling them only with your fair hands, not with just any old hand. You're not calling "to keep them honest," you're calling only when your hand has a good enough chance of winning in relation to the size of the pot that you'll show a long-term profit.

Here's a good rule of thumb: If you *never* get bluffed out of a pot, it's almost certain you're calling too much.

The other extreme is getting so snake-bitten that you fold your fair hands whenever someone raises, or in some cases, reraises. This is especially a problem when you're head-up against an aggressive player. If he sees that you habitually give his raises too much respect by folding all but your very best hands, he may start raising with nothing. This is called *running over* someone who's playing *weak-tight*.

Against such a player, you'll have to call more often than you might prefer. You don't have to *always* call—just often enough that he knows he can't count on disposing of you as easily as that.

Talk Like a Texan

A player who folds too readily, or who only bets his very strong hands while playing tightly and passively otherwise, is said to be **weak-tight.** This is one of the worst insults one poker buff can hurl at another. On the other hand, many poker experts contend that learning how to play weak-tight is the first step toward playing well, since it means you are at least being selective about which hands to play.

Handling Emotion

One of the ironies of Hold'em is that we spend all this time learning highly rational strategies, when the game itself inspires the most irrational of behaviors. This is to our advantage when other people behave irrationally, but alas, few of us are free from the same curse.

Broadly speaking, letting emotion influence you is called being on *tilt*, or *tilting*. The term presumably comes from pinball: ram a pinball machine too hard with your hip, and the machine shuts down and you lose.

Tilt comes in many forms and just about every Hold'em player has fallen victim to it more than once, even seasoned pros. We'll look first at a fairly subtle example, one that many players wouldn't even recognize as tilt unless they thought about it. After that, we'll examine tilt's broader effects on nearly every aspect of play, along with what you can do about it.

Hanging On to Big Pairs with a Death Grip

Say you raise pre-flop with a pair of black Aces and get several callers. The flop comes T♥9♥8♣, so you bet with confidence. To your surprise, a normally timid player raises and a third player calls. You reraise and both players call. The turn adds another Heart. The flop raiser bets again—but this time, the third player raises! What to do?

If you're like most beginners, you're so loath to fold your overpair that you call both the raise and the reraise, and perhaps, another raise and reraise on the river. The first raiser shows a set of Tens, whereupon the second raiser shows the King-Queen of Hearts for the flush and takes all the chips. You sit there mumbling to yourself about Aces being a terrible hand.

The problem here isn't that you truly believe Aces can never lose; it's that you're overly attached to them. And attachment, as practitioners of Buddhism would be quick to remind us, is a form of emotion. Therefore, when you call down in this sort of situation, you've let emotion get the better of you.

This specific instance of tilt has a fairly easy remedy: Learn to recognize that a big pair is just another Hold'em hand. Your goal is to play all of your hands as well as possible. You should eventually be able to let go of pocket Aces that you recognize to be losing just as easily as you'd throw away any other losing hand.

Tilting Full-Blown at Any Windmill

In its most nefarious forms, tilt has you charging hard at everything, winning nothing. Let's say you suffer a *bad beat* when your set of Jacks is drawn out on by a player who makes a straight, but who you feel wasn't justified in calling your pre-flop raise with his horrible cards.

Talk Like a Texan

A **bad beat** occurs when you've got a strong hand that you're playing correctly, only to lose to an opponent who played poorly but overtook you. An example might be when you raise pre-flop with AK, make top pair on the flop, but lose to someone who makes an improbable two pair with a hand like 82s—a hand he probably shouldn't have called your pre-flop raise with. Although some players use the term to refer to any particularly dismaying loss, this is incorrect.

You are furious. Without realizing it, you start playing hands you'd normally throw away. You start bluffing calling stations, something you never do. And on and on it goes. You are on tilt.

This is an extreme example, but unfortunately a very common one. Even when you're not actually angry, nearly any emotion at all can hurt your play. If you feel great at having just scooped a pot, you may loosen up and start playing any two cards, believing that you're on a roll.

Or let's say you take another bad beat, but this time, instead of loosening up, you do the reverse—you tighten up and start throwing away decent hands you'd normally play for a small profit. Smart opponents, recognizing what's happening to you, may take advantage by running you over with bluffs.

How to combat tilt? Like everything else, it takes practice, but here's some ideas to get you started:

- **Be aware of your emotions as you play.** An easy way to do this is to pause occasionally in the moment before it's your turn to act. Use that extra second or two to check in on your feelings.

- **Think about how you'd play if you weren't feeling this way.** For example, if you sense you're about to raise out of anger or a desire for revenge, take an extra moment to consider how you'd play your hand if you *weren't* so angry.

- **Take frequent breaks.** Whether you're playing at a casino or online, there's no rule that says you have to stay at the table, playing hand after hand while you're in a rage. Get up, walk around, go for a stroll. If

you're playing with a buddy, talk over how
you're feeling and how you're playing.

- **Concentrate on playing your best, not
on winning or losing.** It's a strange thing,
but the more desperately you want to win
chips, the worse you'll probably play.
Conversely, the less attention you pay to
how you're doing, the more you can focus
on playing each hand well. You'll learn more
about this approach in Chapter 10.

- **Remember that past events don't affect
the next hand.** You'll hear players say a seat
is cold, or that they never win against a certain other player or with a certain hand.
Don't let their superstition infect you! You
know full well that the cards you get are
random and that the odds don't change
because you're ahead or behind. If you flip a
coin ten times, you might flip seven heads
and three tails. That doesn't change the fact
that it's still a 50-50 proposition on the next
flip.

- **Have a fall-back strategy.** We've warned
against changing your strategy when you're
shaken up—and we've also warned that you
may be better off taking a break or even
quitting for the day. But if you insist on
continuing to play, tightening up is far
better than loosening up. For example, it
wouldn't be terrible to play only your very
best starting hands for a while. The idea is
to avoid having to make difficult decisions
until you regain confidence.

The Least You Need to Know

- Avoid mistakes such as forgetting the pot size by developing good Hold'em habits— for example, by practicing counting the pot when you're not in hands.

- When it comes to questions such as when to bluff, when to call, and when to fold, avoid extremes such as "never" and "always"; instead, make your decision based on your opponent and the situation.

- To keep tilt at bay, practice counter-strategies such as monitoring your feelings, taking breaks, and concentrating on playing your best rather than winning chips.

Chapter 7

Advanced Lessons

In This Chapter

- Introducing the semi-bluff
- Common types of players
- Common types of games
- Hand-reading and tells

We've come a long way but there's much, much more to learn about Hold'em. In this chapter, we introduce you to some more advanced strategies.

If you have a good handle on starting hands, basic odds, and strategy, you're probably ready to start adjusting your play to individual players and specific game situations. If you're brand new to Hold'em though, some of this chapter will probably feel overwhelming.

That's okay—you'll work with these concepts as long as you play the game. There's plenty of time to master them as you gain more experience.

Semi-Bluffing Gives You Two Ways to Win

When you bet with what you think is the best hand, you're trying to win money from players who call. And when you bluff, you're trying to win the whole pot by getting everyone to fold. But what if you bluff with a hand that could also win?

If that doesn't make sense, consider a situation like the following: pre-flop, everyone folds to the dealer; he raises, the small blind folds, and you call in the big blind with a fairly weak hand, 76s. You know there's a good chance the dealer is trying to steal here, opening so late. The other thing you know about him is that he's aggressive, but not very imaginative.

The flop comes 258 giving you a straight draw. He bets, you call. The flop is small enough that if he raised with a bare Ace and not much else, he's only winning by an Ace-high here.

Now the turn comes a T. You can consider checking to him and raising if he bets.

This is a classic *semi-bluff*. Notice that you've got two ways to win here: First if he does hold a weak hand like Ace-high, he may fold outright. Even AK can't be looking too strong to him once you raise. In that case, you win a pot that in most cases would have been his if he'd called you down. Second, even if he *does* call, you still have a 1 in 6 chance of making your straight and beating him on the river. If you miss, you'll just check and fold if he bets since your 7-high isn't likely to be a winner.

Sure, you might make the same play with no draw at all, on a pure bluff. But because the semi-bluff has greater expectation, you can semi-bluff much more often than you can bluff, and with greater confidence. You can raise where some players would just call, and bet where they would check. Your opponents will have a harder time reading your hand and be less likely to bluff into you, knowing you're more likely to *play back* than other players.

Talk Like a Texan

Smart, aggressive players often **play back** by raising or reraising head-up, especially when they smell a bluff or a steal attempt. Usually they play back when they have outs—meaning their raise or reraise is a semi-bluff with some chance of actually winning. A passive player, by contrast, seldom plays back—he's happy to fold if he doesn't hold a definite hand. Which of these two types would you rather have as *your* opponent?

Semi-bluffs are most often employed against just one opponent. And usually they involve hands like straights or flushes, as we've seen. But any play at all where you bet, raise, or check-raise with a hand that can improve to win is considered a semi-bluff, as long as there's some chance your opponent may fold.

Keep in mind that the more likely an opponent is to fold, the less of a hand you need to semi-bluff with; the more likely he is to call, the better your hand should be.

Raise It Up

Comments along the lines of "How could you play that way?!" are common at the table. When you're the target, you may be tempted to set the record straight by reciting your outs or the odds the pot was offering you. Don't! Instead, ignore the question, or answer with a joke or polite evasion. Why let the other players know your strategy—or that you have a strategy at all?

Who Are These Guys?

Hold'em would be very dull (and very expensive) if your opponents played perfectly. Fortunately, most of them will make lots of mistakes, usually centering around their style of play—for example, too passive, too loose, or both. Here's a look at the most common types of players you'll encounter:

- **Les Gamble.** Les is *loose-aggressive*—he likes to raise and bluff a lot. It's good to have Les seated to your right, so you can see his bets coming. When you think you have him beat, you can take advantage by raising to pressure players with so-so hands or draws. Les bets his strong hands, his medium hands, and sometimes his weak hands, too. So you're going to have to call him more, especially when you're head-up.

- **Loose Lucy.** Lucy is *loose-passive*, donating freely by calling with any hand at all and rarely betting or raising. When she *does* come to life with a bet or raise, she's usually got a very big hand—so you don't have to call unless you've got a monster yourself. Be sure to bet for value against her, but don't bother to bluff; Lucy lives to call you down.

- **Slippery Sal.** Sal is loose, too, but he's also tricky. He plays hands like 56s and J3s and has been known to call three bets pre-flop with 22. While bad habits like these make him a long-term loser, Sal does have good card sense. He's capable of strong plays like semi-bluff raising on the turn. And the wide range of hole cards he'll play make it hard to know which cards help him. Sal is aware of how opponents play, so you'll need to consider what he thinks of you. For example, if you've folded a hand or two to raises, it's more likely he'll try a bluff if the two of you are head-up.

Watch Your Chips

It's important to remember that real players aren't as easy to pigeonhole as the stereotyped opponents described here. And the same player can change his battle plan dramatically, depending on factors such as his state of mind, whether he's winning or losing—or even a conscious decision to mix things up.

- **Earnest Reader.** Ernie, as his friends call him, knows how to play *tight*—at least when he first sits down. He's fresh out of college, has read some poker books, and wants to play the "right" way. But in the heat of battle, he sometimes slips and plays more like Les or Lucy than the expert he hopes to become. Watch the size of Ernie's stack, and his mood, as the game progresses, and adjust your calling and raising requirements against him accordingly.

- **Weak Willie.** Willie is *weak-tight*: afraid of the nuts! If a flush or straight is possible, he's sure someone must have it. He'll tend to fold all but his best hands to a bet or raise, regardless of pot odds or whether he's head-up. Willie isn't around as much as he used to be these days, except at the very lowest limits. Players like Les and Sal are just too hard for him to beat. When you do encounter Willie, you can bluff more—and fold weak hands with confidence if he fires back.

- **Mr. and Ms. Chips.** You guessed it—these are the folks who neither call too much, nor fold too often. They patiently wait for good hole cards and adjust their play, depending on opponents, pot odds, and card odds. Just like the other players we've described, they make mistakes and have losing nights. But unlike the others, they've also got the know-how to win more often than not—and to keep improving. You want to *be* Mr. or Ms. Chips, not play against them.

What Kind of Game Is This?

When you put 10 players around a table, their different playing styles combine to give the game a *texture*, as it's called in poker parlance. Smart players adjust to different games; bad players never adjust.

Let's look at some common types of games. As we do, keep in mind that, like the imaginary players we just discussed, these games are stereotypes. In real life, you need to play each hand on a case-by-case basis. For example, even the loosest tables have an occasional head-up pot. And remember, too, that in a crowded cardroom (or online site) with players coming and going, a table can undergo dramatic mood swings in the course of a few hands.

Loose-Aggressive Tables

Put a couple of raise-happy opponents at the same table and rock'em, sock'em action is likely to follow. It's not uncommon to have raises and reraises before and on the flop, with the action slowing on the turn and river.

Tighten Up Before the Flop ...

You need to be extra selective about starting hands in this type of game, folding more draws than usual. Such hands don't do well when the pot is constantly getting raised and reraised before you can see if the flop will help or not.

If you're in late position, you'll be better able to judge how many raises and opponents you'll face, and thus can sneak in a few more drawing hands. But otherwise, favor hands like 99 and higher for pocket pairs, big suited cards like KQs, and possibly a prime drawing hand like JTs for just one raise.

... and Loosen Up After

With so many players calling two or more bets pre-flop, the pot will be big enough that you can pursue many hands you'd normally throw away—inside straight draws, overcards, even middle or bottom pair.

For example, say you hold JTs and end up seeing the flop with five other players for a bet and a raise. The flop comes 38Q, giving you an inside straight draw. It's checked to the button; he bets, gets two callers, and it's your turn. Normally you'd fold, but here you've got an easy call: with four Nines to give you the nut straight, your odds to see the turn are 11 to 1, and the pot is offering you better than that at 15 to 1.

Or say you were the pre-flop raiser with AK on that same flop. Your odds of hitting an Ace or King on the next card are about 7.5 to 1—so you could call a bet and even a raise here. Moreover, you could even bet out here yourself, on the slim possibility that everyone missed this ragged flop and will fold. (Remember semi-bluffing?)

In a loose-aggressive game, the big pots and ups and downs can make you feel like you're on a roller coaster. Stay patient, and concentrate on keeping the odds in your favor. You can be losing after hours of frustrating folds and missed draws, then become a big winner by dragging one huge pot.

Loose-Passive Tables

When four or more players routinely see the flop without a raise, it's an invitation to play many more drawing hands than usual. You can safely limp baby pairs and small suited connectors even under the gun, knowing you'll usually get lots of limpers behind you and no raise. Most of the time you'll miss the flop and quietly fold. But those times you connect, you'll generally get plenty of calls and win a fair-size pot.

The Odds Favor Draws ...

Let's say it's a $2-$4 game, and you limp in with
pocket Deuces against five opponents. Your
chances of flopping a set are about 8 to 1 against,
while your immediate pot odds are only 5 to 1.
But your real odds are your implied odds, as
follows:

> We can hypothesize that three of your oppo-
> nents will call a $2 bet on the flop if a Deuce
> does fall; two will likely call a $4 turn bet; and
> at least one will call the $4 river bet. That
> works out to 14-to-1 odds on your $2 initial
> bet. Here's another way to look at this: seven
> times you won't hit a set and you'll fold, losing
> $2 each time for a total of negative $14. The
> eighth time, you'll hit your set and hopefully
> win $28. If you do the math as discussed in
> Chapter 3, it works out to a positive expecta-
> tion of $1.24 every time you limp those
> Deuces.

> Of course, it isn't that simple. Sometimes
> there'll be a raise behind you and you'll pay
> more to see the flop. About 20 percent of the
> time you'll hit your set and lose anyway. All of
> this chips away at your expectation—but you're
> still getting the best of it when you can come
> in cheaply with hands like these.

... But Big Cards Win Less Often

A penalty for getting a crack at so many cheap draws is that your very best starting hands will lose more often than in a tighter game. For example, you can raise with AA, get five callers, and lose when some *fish* who called your raise with K7s makes a flush, or a hand like 54 makes two pair.

Talk Like a Texan

A **fish** refers to an unskilled, losing Hold'em player. The more the game you're in resembles an aquarium, the better for you in the long run. When the fish are schooling, though, the short run can be frustrating. In a game full of piscine players, there's always a good chance someone will take down your AK with K2 when the flop comes K22. Just remember, the guy playing K2 against AK is going to get filleted more often than not.

Does that mean you shouldn't raise your big pairs? Absolutely not. You'll win less often, but you'll still be a money favorite. For example, if you raise with AA and get five callers to the flop, you've contributed less than 17 percent to the pot—but your Aces are a favorite to win a third of the time or more.

What's more, you don't always have to call to the end with your big pair. Learning to recognize situations where the cards on board and the betting action make a fold prudent can save you a lot of bets.

For example, if you hold A♦A♥, the flop comes 89T with all Clubs, and there's a bet and a raise, you can usually fold. This goes back to the idea of reverse implied odds in Chapter 3: Even if your opponents haven't flopped a straight or flush outright, they've got too many ways of beating you, and you've got hardly any ways to improve to beat them.

Watch Your Chips

It's fine to be cautious with big pairs in tricky spots, but don't overdo it. In the previous example, a fold is in order—but against a slightly less scary board, or if there hadn't been a raise, a call would often be the better play. This is one instance of a more general principle in limit poker: folding errors versus calling errors. Calling just one or two more bets in a big pot is a small error—but folding and losing an entire pot that should have been yours is a disaster!

Should you still raise before the flop with offsuit big-card hands like AK and AQ? Yes with AK—but not always with AQ. If six limpers have entered the pot and you're on the button with AQ, you're not doing yourself any favors by raising—this is a hand that prefers few opponents. Keep the pot as small as possible by just calling, and wait to see if you flop good.

Weaker offsuit hands like AJ and AT are even less tenable against a crowd. These hands scream for just a couple of opponents to be successful, and that's not what you're going to get here. Expert players often throw them away in a very loose-passive game, when they'd be raising with them in a tight game.

Tight-Passive Tables

It's unusual to find a very tight low-limit Hold'em—playing too many hands seems to be a more common mistake than playing too few. But tight tables are out there, and you can do very well against a bunch of tight types as long as they also play fairly passively.

With fewer opponents than usual, drawing hands go down in value and high cards go up. The semi-bluff is also more valuable. When you're the first player in, you can raise pre-flop in middle position with terribly weak hands such as 44 or A9s. First in from late position, you can raise with as little as K10 or A5.

In this manner you can run over the game by winning lots of small pots. It's easy to bluff if the other players only call or raise when they have strong hands.

Tight-Aggressive Tables

When play at a table is tight but aggressive, it's much harder to win. Now lots of pots will be played head-up or three-way, but the players will semi-bluff their draws, slow-play big hands, value bet into your draws, and play back at you when they think you're bluffing.

In short, tight-aggressive tables aren't very profitable because the other players are playing too well. Luckily, your best strategy the few times you find yourself at a table like this is obvious: look for a better game.

Hand-Reading and Tells

As you become a better Hold'em player, you'll begin to be able to deduce possible hands your opponents may hold. By combining general knowledge about a player with the board and the action, you can often read the hands he's likely to be holding.

Example 1

Here's a simple example. You raise pre-flop with J♣J♠ in middle position. Les Gamble and Loose

Lucy both call. Now the flop comes A♦4♦5♣. You bet, Les raises, and Lucy calls. You also call. The turn card is the 2♦. You check, Les bets, Lucy raises. What now?

Knowledge of your opponents tells you this is an easy fold. While Les is capable of betting without an Ace, Lucy almost certainly wouldn't raise without the goods—probably either two Diamonds for the flush, or even a trey for the straight. She's a loose player, and it's perfectly possible she called your pre-flop raise with a hand like 8♦Q♦ or 33.

Example 2

Slippery Sal limps and you raise on the button holding A9. Earnest Reader calls in the big blind and Sal calls, too. The flop comes 10♠9♥5♠; Earnie checks, and Sal bets. You raise as a semi-bluff with what may or may not be the best hand, and although Earnie folds, Sal calls. The turn card is the 6♣; Sal checks and calls your bet. The river brings the 2♦, and Sal again checks to you. What's your move?

This time, your knowledge of Sal and your read of the action suggests putting in one more bet. Being aggressive, Sal wouldn't have passed up a check-raise on the turn if he had a big hand—so there's a good chance he's gotten trapped with something relatively weak. Maybe he's got two Spades and will simply fold to your bet. Maybe he has a hand like 10♦8♦ and will call and beat you. But there's also a good chance he's holding a little pair like 44, suited cards like J♠6♠ that missed the flush but paired on the turn, or even two overcards. When that's the case, he often calls and you collect an extra bet.

Watch Your Chips

Don't fall into the trap of reading opponents for one specific hand. Instead, think in terms of possible hands a player might have based on how they play and on their actions throughout this particular hand. For example, you could tentatively put an opponent who just calls on a two-suited flop on a flush draw. But be ready adjust your assessment if he or she suddenly gets aggressive on the turn even though a third suited card is nowhere in sight.

What Are the Players Telling You?

If you've seen the movie *Rounders*, you probably remember the scene where Matt Damon's Mike McDermott picks up a tell on his primary opponent, Teddy KGB. Teddy likes to eat Oreos while he plays high-stakes Hold'em, and Mike notices he only eats the cream when he has something strong. By observing this cookie tell, Mike avoids a heavy loss with a well-timed fold.

Watching for giveaway actions like this can help you, too, but not as often as you might think. If you're playing online, tells are pretty much non-existent. And in live games, you won't always know whether a stranger's shaking hand is due to excitement, age, or too much coffee.

Still, there are many common tells worth knowing about. Here are a few examples:

- When the flop is dealt, most players will be watching the cards. You can watch their faces instead. A player who glances quickly from the board to her chips may have hit something strong. A player who continues staring at the board may be disappointed by what he sees.

- Occasionally you can detect an impending bet or raise by watching for naïve players who unconsciously pick up chips before the action gets to them. On the other hand, some players grab chips anytime they intend to call. You've got to watch until you know who's who and what their habits are.

- Body language can speak volumes. For example, if someone who was slumping sits up a little straighter when he sees the flop, something good has probably happened for his hand. But such body language should be subtle: anything blatant is usually an act put on for your benefit.

- A player who talks to an opponent after betting may be trying to coax him into calling. Tricky players do this often—because it often works!

The Least You Need to Know

- Playing "by the book" isn't enough—winning players use advanced strategies to adjust to different opponents and types of games.

- A semi-bluff gives you two ways to win: one if everyone folds, the other if you're called and your hand improves enough to take the pot.

- By categorizing opponents along the lines of loose, tight, passive, or aggressive, you can more easily profit from their errors.

- Games also fall into types such as loose or tight, passive or aggressive. The key here is to watch for how many people usually enter the pot, and how often they raise.

- Hand-reading is the skill of figuring out a range of likely hole cards for an opponent based on her playing style, the betting action, and the board.

Chapter 8

No-Limit and Tournament Hold'em

In This Chapter

- Adjusting to no-limit
- Tournament tips and types
- Cash game considerations
- No-limit quiz

The champion frowns at the flop. After a brooding pause, he detaches three monster stacks of chips and pushes them gently forward, using just his fingertips. The challenger, a much younger man, bounces nervously in his seat—then with a sweeping gesture pushes his entire stack into the pot.

That's right—it's no-limit Hold'em, and our hero has just gone *all-in*. If the champion calls, they'll both flip up their hands. As the crowd holds its breath, the dealer will burn and turn the final two community cards before declaring the winner.

You just don't get that kind of rush in limit poker. That may be one reason why no-limit is such a natural for television and the movies. It also helps explain the craze for easily affordable no-limit tournaments and cash games in cardrooms and on Internet poker sites over the last few years. Everybody wants to be Matt Damon or Doyle Brunson or Annie Duke—take your pick.

In case our example didn't make it clear, in no-limit you can bet any number of chips, up to everything you have on the table. Good no-limit players combine a firm grasp of strategy and odds, an instinct for sizing up opponents, and the courage to risk it all at any time—even on a stone-cold bluff. Or should we say, *especially* on a stone-cold bluff.

This requirement for an oversized heart, along with Svengali-like skills at mind reading and manipulation, is why Doyle Brunson once described the game as "the Cadillac of poker." But even for ordinary mortals, it can be lots of fun if you play for small stakes—and learning your no-limit ABC's will help.

We look at no-limit from three points of view: First, some general differences between no-limit and limit; second, how to play no-limit tournaments (perhaps the most popular form of the game today); and third and last, how to play in regular, nontournament no-limit games.

General No-limit Guidelines

Perhaps the biggest difference between limit and no-limit is that in limit, players often get a good price with drawing hands. But in no-limit, someone holding a big pair or two big cards can raise enough to wreck the pot odds for drawing hands, forcing them to fold pre-flop or on the flop.

As a result, no-limit sees fewer multi-way pots and more head-up or three-way pots. Let's look at the implications of this.

Make the Right-Size Bet or Raise

Just because you can bet any amount in no-limit doesn't mean you should. This is especially true before the flop.

Say you're in early position with a strong but vulnerable hand like AK or QQ. Usually, your best move is to raise about four times the big blind. Why not just shove all your money in? First, if no one has a monster to play back with, you're only going to win the blinds. Second, if someone *does* match up chips, they likely have the ultimate monster, AA—in which case you can go ahead and slap your cards on a stick and hold them over a campfire. What you want is to knock out the draws, while admitting big-card hands just a little worse than your own.

How about when you're holding a big pair, but several people have already limped in or called a modest raise? In that case, you'll want to measure your protective raise against the current size of the pot rather than against the big blind.

A good example would be if you're holding KK on the button in a game with two $5 blinds. A player in middle position raises to $25 and two more call. With $85 in the pot, you might choose to raise to $200 to protect your hand. Now the other players are getting much worse pot odds to see the flop and people who might have drawn out on you with mediocre hands may be forced to fold.

 Watch Your Chips

If you've seen poker tournaments on TV, you've probably noticed players going all in with mediocre hands, or even awful ones. What isn't always clear is the reason why. Generally, you're seeing action from the late stages of a tournament, where high blinds and antes basically force players to gamble. In cash games or early rounds of tournaments there's no need to play this way. In fact, doing so can be extremely costly when someone who *does* have a hand calls your bluff.

Pick Your Spots to Bluff

Fewer opponents plus the ability to put an opponent's entire stack at risk means many more bluffs than in limit poker. The best bluffers are extraordinarily talented at reading people, but it's also a skill that you can work on developing.

Start by getting as completely into your opponent's head as possible. This includes not only how he views himself, but how he views you. Remember the hands you've played together: Have they left him with the impression you bet only the nuts, or does he think you're a loosey-goosey? Does he have any betting patterns that might indicate weakness or strength?

As for semi-bluffing, this, too, gains extra value in no-limit, although it may be more appropriate to think of it as "bluffing with outs," because the bluff is often the main reason for your play. For example, if you flop middle pair and an inside straight draw, you might overbet the pot if you're head-up. You're hoping to scare your opponent into folding, but if he calls, you can still hit a straight, trips, or two-pair.

Don't Pay Through the Nose for a Draw

Calling a small bet pre-flop in hopes of hitting a drawing hand is fine: if you hit the flop, you've got the potential to get deep into someone's stack. So your implied odds are excellent.

But remember that draws go out the window in the face of a heavy raise—now your implied odds aren't likely to be nearly as high. And, even if you do get lucky enough to actually hit your draw, a smart opponent is likely to see this and fold rather than pay you off.

Think Two Bets Ahead

Before you bet, call, or raise, think about what you'd like to have happen next. If you have a set of Aces against an aggressive opponent, you could put out a small feeler bet. You're hoping he'll think you're weak and raise. Then you can spring your trap and reraise, giving him the choice of abandoning a nice chunk of his stack or getting in even deeper.

Here's another example of planning ahead: Say you're down to your last $30 in a nontournament game and you flop a draw to the nut straight with four other players in. Your play here is to check, hoping someone else will make a small bet. If several players call, you'll then go all-in. If everyone folds to your all-in, that would be fine; but if they call, that'll be okay, too: the odds are only a little worse than 2 to 1 against hitting your straight on the turn or river.

Tournament Tips

One of the nice things about tournaments is that even though it's no-limit, you can't lose *all* your money—just your buy-in. On the other hand, neither can you get up and cash out when you're ahead. You must play on until you either win or get eliminated. If you *do* win, however, you'll walk away with a vastly larger sum than the one you put at risk.

Chips Change in Value

For tournaments, you buy in for a specific amount and get tournament chips in return. These chips have mock dollar values that apply only to the tournament. Their real value comes from how much of a share in the prize pool they could give you.

For example, say you enter a $50 buy-in tournament and get $500 in tournament chips. You reach the final table, where it comes down to you and two opponents. They each have $24,000 in tournament chips, but you have just $2,000. The prize structure, meanwhile, is $1,600 for first place, $800 for second, and $400 for third. Even though you only have 4 percent of the chips, you're guaranteed to win at least 14.3 percent of the money!

The lesson here is that at every stage, you need to constantly think about conserving or maximizing your chips so as to finish as high up in the money as possible. Perversely, the fewer chips you have, the more value each chip has on a per-chip basis.

Start Tight, Gamble Late

In tournaments, the blinds start small and get bigger at set intervals. For example, in our $50 buy-in tournament the blinds might start at $5-$10 and move up from there. The idea is that rising blinds force the action, keeping players from just sitting on their chips waiting for premium hands.

In this type of structure, you'll want to play tight in the early going. Let the other players fight for the lead and knock each other out. The more players who are eliminated early, the fewer opponents you'll have to battle later. You certainly want to avoid going all-in early unless you have the nuts or very close to it, along with a chance to win a big pot.

As the blinds rise, you'll be forced to mix it up more. You do this by trying to steal small pots wherever possible, in addition to playing any quality hands you manage to catch. In our example tournament, you might reach this stage with blinds of $50-$100 and a stack of $800. As the pots get bigger, you will have to be more willing to go all-in. In general, if you're going to bet or call for over 50 percent of your stack, you should seriously consider going all-in instead.

Later still, the blinds will get so big in relation to your stack that you may have to go all-in on any reasonable hand—in some cases no more than Ace-high. Other players will be feeling the same pressure, and may raise or call a raise even with weak cards. Unless you've got a huge chip lead, survival becomes a matter of stealing blinds, pushing weaker holdings, picking off bluffs, and being lucky enough to catch a few monsters at the right time.

Raise It Up

Most tournaments allow players at the final table to negotiate a division of the prize pool. Usually everyone must agree for a deal to take place, so estimates of playing ability figure in as well as stack sizes.

Go for Knockouts

Once you survive the opening stages of a tournament, the value of knocking out other players rises. Imagine you started out in a $25 buy-in tournament with 100 players, and it's now down to just 30. Only the top 10 will finish in the money, so each player you can bust out puts you a step closer. It's even more important at the final table: if tenth place pays $40 and ninth place pays $80, knocking out even a single player at least doubles your earnings!

This means that players with big stacks should be bullies, constantly forcing players with smaller stacks to either fold or go all-in. Small stacks, meanwhile, should avoid confrontations while holding out for the occasional steal or for good cards, and a chance to double-up.

To Rebuy or Not to Rebuy?

In addition to the initial buy-in, many tournaments allow rebuys—purchases of additional chips during the first half-hour or hour of play. Some tournaments limit how many rebuys you can make, while others permit unlimited rebuys.

In some tournaments, rebuys cost less per chip than the initial buy-in. In these sorts of "progressive stack" rebuy tournaments, those who rebuy gain at the expense of those who don't.

In most tournaments, though, additional chips cost the same as the original buy-in. Rebuys are therefore only a bargain if they'll make a real difference. For example, if a lot of players were knocked out early and you've managed to accumulate a medium-size stack, it may be worthwhile to rebuy, because your chances of winning have improved considerably.

Tournament Types

If you want to play in the World Championship at the World Series of Poker, you'll have to come up with $10,000 for the buy-in. At the other end of the financial spectrum there are tournaments online you can play for $5 or less.

You probably don't need help choosing the right buy-in size, but tournament structures can vary almost as widely as the stakes. Here's a quick guide to help you sort out the choices.

Build Your Stack

The most famous no-limit tournament is the so-called World Championship, the centerpiece of the annual World Series of Poker. The first championship was actually made up of a rotation of five games, including no-limit Hold'em, with the famous Johnny Moss declared the winner by vote of the players. The next year, 1971, the championship event was restricted to just no-limit Hold'em. Only five players competed, and Moss won again. The championship has grown a bit since then—in 2004, there were 2,577 entrants, and champion Greg Raymer won $5,000,000.

No-Limit Tournaments

This is the type of multi-table tournament we've been discussing so far, with rising blinds and payout amounts based on the total entry fees and rebuys, minus the sponsor's fee. Typically, everyone at the final table finishes "in the money," with first and second place earning the lion's share.

Limit Tournaments

In limit Hold'em tournaments, the blinds go up—and because this is limit poker, so do the limits.

The steady increases have the same effect on strategy as in a no-limit tournament, forcing the action and increasing the tension between players with tall stacks and those with short ones.

You may be tempted to play drawing hands in a limit tournament, just as in a regular game—but this is tenable only in the very early stages, when the limits are still low. Quite soon drawing hands become junk: by their nature they'll usually lose in any single confrontation, and you need to be wary of chasing in hopes of a big score when you can't replace your chips.

 Watch Your Chips _____

> When a tournament gets down to just a few players above those who'll receive prize money, those few players are said to be "on the bubble." If it's you on the bubble, try to dodge big confrontations; that way, you can squeak into the money by default as others get knocked out. But also look for players who are playing it *too* safe—you may get chances to bluff.

Satellites

Eric Drache, who ran the World Series of Poker for many years, is credited with having invented smaller "satellite" tournaments in the early 1980s, to expand the field for the main event. The idea was that a satellite could charge a few dozen players $500 each and award a $10,000 seat in the World Series of Poker to the winner. That gave players who couldn't afford the regular ten grand buy-in a shot at the championship for a bargain price.

Recently, online poker sites have taken this concept even further. With thousands of players participating, satellite entry fees are frequently less than 50 dollars.

Sit and Gos

These one-table events are sometimes offered live but are especially popular online, where the buy-in can range from $5 to $25 per player. As the name suggests, once the table is full, the tournament begins. They're a good way to get a feel for tournament play without investing a lot of time or money. Fewer entrants increase your chances of finishing in the money, but, of course, they also decrease the amount you can win.

Shootouts

These are multi-table tournaments with a twist. In a normal tournament, as players get knocked out, the survivors are reseated, so that tables are always as full as possible. But in a shootout, players stay at their initial table until a single winner emerges victorious. The individual winners from each table then convene on the final table to thrash it out.

No-Limit Strategy for Cash Games

If you're playing no-limit in a nontournament game, or *cash game*, you'll rely on the same general principles to guide your play: bet and raise the right amounts, be wary of draws, and so on. The differences are these: first, your chips represent ordinary cash, not a chance at a prize pool; and second, since you can't get eliminated, only your wallet and your common sense determine when you quit playing.

Aim for a Few Big Pots

Obviously, the blinds don't go up in a cash game as they do in a tournament, either. When you sit down in a $1-$2 no-limit game, that's what you'll be playing for as long as you're at the table. So there's never pressure to play an inferior hand because rising blinds are eating away at your stack.

A good strategy for most cash games is to play about the same as you would in the early rounds of a tournament. You want to win a few big pots, not a bunch of small ones. And every now and then you want to exploit your tight image to make a well-timed bluff.

Make sure you know how much the other players have in front of them. You might consider calling a medium-size bet from a player with a big stack, in hopes you'll hit your hand and be able to win a big pot. Against a player with only a few chips, though, the potential pot odds won't be there.

Limit Your Risk

You should be watching your own stack, too. While you'll want to keep enough in front of you to be able to overbet fair-size pots, don't buy in for more than you can live with losing. In a cash game with $1 and $2 blinds, a $200 buy-in will give you plenty of leverage.

You can't play no-limit without being ready to go all-in, and there's no shame in losing everything you have on the table. You can come back with a big win without playing loosely or trying to win lots of pots. All it takes is one winning hand where you get all your chips in to double your stake.

Don't judge how well you're playing based on the turn of the cards in a few monster pots. Instead, focus on consistently having an edge whenever you put significant chips at risk.

For example, if you go all-in with AK against 99 before the flop, you're a slight underdog—about 13-to-10 against. But get your chips in with AA against that same 99, and you're a 2-1 favorite. In the latter case, you'll know you made the right play, even those times when the other guy gets lucky and takes all your chips.

Quiz on No-Limit Play

Let's finish up with three quick no-limit questions:

> **Q:** It's the second round of a tournament. Only a few players have gone out so far. You've been

playing tight and have only a few more chips than you started with. Now you're dealt TT under the gun. What should you do?

A: The blinds are still low at this stage, and you hold a vulnerable hand. There's nothing wrong with just limping in here and hoping several others come along to give you action if you hit your set. Raising only a small amount, like double the big blind, won't pose much of a deterrent. And raising more, say four times the blind, would be risking too much of your stack for not enough reward, especially with the entire table yet to act. If someone makes a big bet after you limp, you can throw your Tens away without having lost much.

Q: You're at the final table and hold A9 on a flop of AQ4 with two of a suit. Two other players are in. One has a short stack, the other has about the same amount of chips as you. The short stack goes all-in and you're next to act. Call, raise, or fold?

A: A big raise might maximize your chances of winning the pot by knocking out the third player. But a call could be the better play here. If just calling allows the other player to stay in, he could possibly knock out the all-in player if you don't, moving you both up the payout ladder. Furthermore you could avert a potentially expensive confrontation with a player who has enough chips to do you serious harm, or even knock you out of the tournament.

Q: You're in a cash game with $1 and $2 blinds, with a bit more than $300 in chips in front of you. You're dealt K♥Q♥ in early position, and raise this big suited hand to $8. To your discomfort, a player you know to be quite tight calls; he's sitting on about $4,400 in chips. The loose and aggressive player in the big blind calls, too. The flop comes A♥8♥3♣. The loose BB checks and you bet $25, about the size of the pot. The tight player thinks for a moment, then fires in a $200 reraise. The big blind folds and it's up to you.

A: Here is where stack sizes matter. In a limit game, you'd certainly be seeing your nut flush draw to the end. But this is no-limit. There's $280 in the pot, so you're getting less than 1.5-to-1 pot odds on a call. What's more, if the flush card doesn't come on the turn, your opponent can set you in for your remaining $100, and the pot odds at that point will force you to call. So you're looking at risking your entire $300 to win a pot of $380. The odds just aren't there. If you don't think this opponent is bluffing, a fold is in order.

The Least You Need to Know

- Unlike limit, in no-limit you can bet as much as you want at any time, up to the full amount you have on the table.

- Gauge the size or your bets and raises by the size of the blinds, the size of the pot, and the pot odds your bet or raise will create for opponents.

- Tournaments force you to alternate between extreme aggression and extreme conservation, as you hoard irreplaceable tournament chips with an eye toward the final table.

- Cash no-limit games encourage a selective strategy, focused on winning just a few big pots, not lots of small ones.

Chapter 9

Online, or Bricks and Mortar?

In This Chapter

- Casino and club checklist
- Online checklist
- Playing shorthanded
- Cheating and other chicanery

Most of this book has been devoted to *how* to play Hold'em. Now we'll look at *where* to play. There have never been more choices: from Internet sites to casinos and from penny stakes to big bucks.

For pros, online poker offers the advantage of playing multiple tables at once, thereby earning more per hour than is possible live. For recreational players, the main advantages are convenience and low stakes.

Playing live has attractions, too. If you work in front of a monitor all day, you may prefer seeing other players and feeling the buzz of a cardroom. And you're more likely to get friendly with fellow newbies in a cardroom than chatting online.

Just as e-mail hasn't eliminated the need for face-to-face contact, the boom in online poker hasn't dented live Hold'em venues. In fact, cardrooms and casinos are booming—and perhaps attracting some players who learned the game online.

Casino and Club Checklist

If you decide to give live play a try, call the nearest casinos or cardrooms and ask what stakes they offer. Generally, the lowest limits are $2-$4, $3-$6, and $1-$3 spread limit.

When you arrive, look for a list of games currently available. In small clubs, it may just be a clipboard; in casinos, it's likely to be a big board showing games, stakes, and the initials of waiting players. Ask for your game of choice. If there's a free seat, you'll be directed to the table. If not, your initials will go on the waiting list, too.

Raise It Up

As you gain experience and skill, there's one crucial factor to consider in choosing your table: locating a *good game*. In poker terms, that means a game where at least one or two of the players are terrible, and where overall you'll be one of the better players. As a general guideline, look for loose games with lots of callers, little raising, and a generally happy mood. It pays to be choosy. Even the tenth-best Hold'em player in the world won't do too well at a table with the top nine.

Rules and Etiquette

Here are a few basics to get you ready:

- **Buy-in amount:** Hold'em games usually have a minimum buy-in. For a $2-$4 game, it might be as little as $20. However, we recommend buying in for 30 big bets—in this case, $120. That gives you enough ammo to last a while. You can get chips at the cashier or at the table, depending on cardroom policy.

- **Posting:** When you first sit down you'll generally have two choices: either "post" the amount of the big blind and get cards right away, or wait until it's your turn to be big blind. If there are only a few hands to go, it's generally more economical to wait. Sometimes, the players on your immediate left and right will ask if you will chop blinds with them—that is take back your forced bets when no one else enters the pot. Whether or not to do so is entirely up to you.

- **Table stakes:** You can only bet money you have on the table in the form of chips and cash—reaching into your wallet isn't allowed until the hand is over. It's frustrating to finally get a good hand and be unable to win the maximum—another good reason to buy in for more than the minimum.

- **Betting:** It's important to wait your turn to call, bet, raise, or fold. It's not just good manners—acting out of turn can wreak havoc by causing some players to change their minds about betting or calling, possibly irritating still other players who'd laid plans of one sort or another. Do your best, but don't worry too much if you slip up a few times: part of the dealer's job is to help newcomers understand what's required.

- **Raising:** If you want to raise, be sure to put the full amount out all at once. Don't place enough to call in front of you and then return to your stack to raise. That's a string bet, and will usually be disallowed. It's a good idea to announce what you're doing each time you act: "Bet," "Call," etc.

Talk Like a Texan

When everyone folds to the blinds, they can opt either to play the hand out, or else **chop** by taking back their blind bets. In many low-stakes games, the house takes a cut out of the pot if a flop is dealt, but not on a chop. That's a pretty powerful point in favor of chopping, but it's always your call. Chopping is a convention, not a rule. Whatever you do, be consistent. Chopping your weak hands but playing your monsters is widely considered to be taking unfair advantage.

- **Looking at your hand:** Look at your cards by separating them slightly and bending them up at one corner, shielding them with your free hand. And never pick up your hand and hold it beyond the table's outside edge—not only is this against the rules in most cardrooms, but it'll firmly brand you as a newbie and easy mark.

- **Protecting your hand:** We mentioned this back in Chapter 2, but it bears repeating: if your hole cards get mixed up with other cards on the table, or if the dealer thinks you've folded and mucks your cards, you're out. As a safeguard, place a chip, coin, or trinket on top of your cards.

- **Declaring your hand:** When two or more players reach a showdown, the last bettor or raiser is required to show his hand first. If at that point you're certain you've lost, it's fine to toss your cards into the muck and keep your own secrets. But if you *aren't* 100 percent sure, go ahead and turn your hand up so the dealer can declare the winner. Even veterans sometimes miss an unlikely straight, flush, or other winning hand.

- **Tipping:** When you win a hand it's customary to tip the dealer—like waiters, they depend on tips for much of their income. At low limits, $1 is usually plenty, although if you win an especially big pot you might make it $2 or more. When you take a tiny pot, it's fine to skip the tip. In cardrooms where dealers get to keep their own tips rather than pool them, we're inclined to be more generous with fast, efficient dealers. If a dealer is slow, rude, or mistake-prone, you needn't tip at all.

- **Customer service:** The *floor* isn't just what you walk on in a cardroom—it's also a catch-all title for middle management. If there's a dispute between players or you want to change tables, you'll need to call the floor.

Online Checklist

Some things are the same online as live, such as posting blinds and table stakes. Others simply don't apply—betting and raising are done by clicking a mouse, and you don't tip the tiny robot dealer inside the software.

Rules and Etiquette

One big difference in online play is that you can't just plunk down cash in exchange for chips. Before you can play you'll have to get funds into an account at your chosen poker site. Most major credit card companies won't allow gambling transactions, nor will some online intermediaries.

If you're comfortable giving a site your bank account information, you may be able to make a direct electronic transfer. We'd recommend that you find an online firm that will act as a middleman for the transaction, instead—a popular way of managing payment on the Internet. If all else fails, you can always mail a bank check or postal money order. Once you've funded your account and are ready to play, here are some useful things to know:

- **Finding a game:** Internet poker software typically lists games in progress. When you find a game at your stakes, just click and you'll be taken to the table.

- **Taking notes:** Almost all online sites let you take electronic notes on other players, which goes a long way toward compensating for the fact you can't see your opponents. Besides telling you who's good and who's a fish, notes can remind you of your adversaries' individual quirks and betting habits.

- **Regulation:** Unlike U.S. casinos, which are almost universally subject to gaming commissions, tribal authorities or other regulatory bodies, online poker sites exist in a shadow world. Running one is illegal in the United States, and all the major sites are operated offshore. Despite this, the large sites have a solid reputation for running honest games, with attention to customer service and no problems cashing out.

Raise It Up

The rake is the house share of each pot. A typical rake in a live $2-$4 game might be two dollars on the flop, a dollar more when the pot reaches $20, and a final dollar at $30. That's a lot of money coming off the table every hand, and a good reason to move up to slightly higher stakes when you can: the rake is often the same dollar amount in the bigger game, and therefore, a smaller percentage. Rakes are generally lower online than live, perhaps due to the faster rate of play and lower overhead.

Playing with Fewer Opponents

Most of the strategy advice in this book has assumed you're sitting at a full table of seven to nine players. But what if it's short-handed? This happens in lulls at cardrooms, at the final table in tournaments, and online, where special tables offer seating for five or at most six players. Many players aren't comfortable short-handed, but if you make the right adjustments, it can be both fun and profitable.

High Cards Go Up in Value

With fewer hands dealt, normally weak hands like AT and KJ become relative powerhouses. Draws, on the other hand, become traps: with a hand like T9s, you want at least four callers to get the right odds, and you'll seldom get this many shorthanded.

Aggression Pays

Forceful play pays off short-handed, so if you're first in, knock the door down with a raise. Many pots are contested head-up or three-way, and the winner tends to be whoever bets first. Unlike full games, where someone usually has a hand, short-handed play is about winning lots of small pots with weaker holdings.

Cheating and Other Bad Behavior

If you're playing in a reputable casino or cardroom or on a well-known Internet site, cheating almost certainly won't happen often enough to affect your results. If you do suspect something, don't be shy—report it to the powers that be. You'll be protecting other players besides yourself.

Collusion

Probably the most common form of cheating occurs when two or more players team up. They can *jam* the pot when one of them has a strong hand, extracting the maximum from anyone trapped in the middle, or use multiple raises to force others to fold.

Colluders don't necessarily make out all that well, though. For one thing, they risk multiplying their losses when an intended victim has a strong hand. For another, collusion can be spotted relatively easily: the operators of online sites even have special computer programs that monitor suspicious betting patterns. These programs are good enough that colluders are taking a real risk of being caught and banned for life.

Marked Cards

Sometimes players will bend or otherwise mark a card so they can spot it later. The cards now used in most public cardrooms are made of tough plastic, so this isn't easy to do. You might be more likely to run into this in a home game. That's also where you might see simple cheating tactics, such as importing extra chips into a game or hiding an Ace.

Angleshooting

Much more common than outright cheating is *angleshooting*—tricks and ploys that are unethical, but not clearly against the rules. Again, if someone persists in angleshooting, don't hesitate to complain to management.

Here are a few common ploys and ways to defend against them:

- **Lying about a hand:** At showdown, some players will say they have a flush or straight when they really don't. Or they may ask if you can beat a particular hand. They're hoping you'll muck, giving them the pot. The solution is simple: protect your cards until they show theirs and the dealer declares their hand.

- **Shorting the pot:** Some players will deliberately put in too few chips, "forget" to put in a bet, or raise or even slip chips out of the pot. The dealer should keep this behavior in check, but if you're at a wild table, keep your eyes open.

- **Peeking at other players' cards:** Knowing another player's hand gives the angleshooter an unfair advantage not only over that player, but everyone else in the game. It's perfectly acceptable to ask the victim to protect his cards.

- **Acting out of turn:** Some players will check or even show their hands before you have a chance to bet, hoping for a free card or showdown. If you want to bet, firmly assert that you hadn't yet acted and stick to your guns.

The Least You Need to Know

- Places to play Hold'em include casinos, cardrooms and Internet sites.

- Online play offers convenience and an opportunity to play lots of hands for very low stakes; live play lets you see opponents, meet other players, and enjoy the ambiance of the cardroom.

- To beat short-handed games, get aggressive with your weaker big-card hands, while playing fewer draws.

- While most players and games are on the level, cheating and unethical behavior do occur. Generally, a little alertness and common sense are all it takes to protect yourself.

10

Having Fun Without Going Broke

In This Chapter
- Variance and bankrolls
- Keeping poker in perspective
- What about going pro?

After seeing your share of flops and raking in a pot or two on the river, you'll likely come to a decision on whether Hold'em is the game for you.

Like golf, chess, and other recreational pursuits, Hold'em can be a lifetime source of pleasure and intellectual stimulation. In this chapter, we offer a few final tips to help you get the most out of the game, while avoiding unnecessary frustration or disappointment.

You should know that even for the best of players, poker is a bumpy ride. Understanding the statistical reasons for this can help make your own ups and downs easier to handle.

Such knowledge helps in other ways, too. Specifically, you'll be better equipped to decide how much money to commit to the game and what sort of stakes to play for. In effect, you're in charge of your own poker economy.

Good economic decisions will be even more vital if you ever consider turning pro or using poker as a source of supplemental income. This may seem unlikely now, but isn't out of the question for someone with a latent talent for the game.

A Random Look at Results

When you're first learning, you expect to lose most of the time. But you may be under the impression that once you get your game together, you'll start winning steadily and never look back.

Unfortunately, it's not quite that simple. Even the best players can suffer losing streaks that last for days, weeks, or months. And although it's rare for a solid player to endure a losing streak of a year or more, it's statistically quite possible.

This has to do with what's generally called *variance*. This is a statistical term that means that any series of results with a random component to them will tend to be scattered above and below their long-term average. In the case of poker, although we know that probabilities apply in the long run, the cards are most assuredly random in the short run.

Build Your Stack

Roy Cooke is a well-known poker pro and writer, specializing in Hold'em. His columns for *CardPlayer Magazine*, offering as they do a painfully honest appraisal of a pro's ups and downs, can make for inspiring reading as you struggle to get your own game together. An additional bonus is getting to peek inside a top player's brain as he makes decisions at the table.

Moreover, the better you get as a player, the bigger your variance. Why? Because you're sitting there waiting for those rare occasions when you have positive expectation. And each time you find one, you're committing as much money as you can by raising, semi-bluffing, and so on. In the long run, this is smart, but in the short run, your results depend on fewer and more heavily weighted events. It's like you're driving on a washboard dirt road leading to a gold mine, but in an old pickup with no shocks. You'll get the gold, but not without some bumps and bruises on the way.

In contrast, most bad players are loose-passive, committing relatively small sums of money to many events—basically, calling with many hands and rarely raising. This results in a nice, smooth pattern of results, like gliding down the road in a fine limousine. Of course, it's also a *losing* pattern, so the limo's destination is not a gold mine, but a cheap motel with no running water and a broken color TV.

Fighting Back with Record-Keeping

What can you do to tame variance? First, and perhaps most essential, you need to find out if you're a winning player.

You do this by keeping detailed records of every session you play. This may sound like a drag, and if you're not up for it, we'll excuse you. But even recreational players find that once they start playing regularly, keeping records actually makes the game more enjoyable, not less.

The essential data to record are location, stakes, session length in hours, and your dollar win or loss. You can do this in a small notebook or however you like. Later, you may want to transfer this information to a spreadsheet to make calculations easier, but that's not a requirement.

After you accumulate enough data, you can start analyzing your performance. How much data is enough? Generally, a couple hundred hours is best, but you can begin calculating before that to get practice. What you're working out is your *hourly rate*—the average amount you win or lose for each hour you play.

Assuming you're playing limit poker, you can take a further step by dividing your hourly rate in dollars by the big bet for the stakes you're playing at. This gives you your hourly rate in big bets per hour. It's handy as a measure of how well you're doing compared to how well you *could* be doing. Basically, if you're beating a limit Hold'em game for one big bet or more, you're on your way to being a winning player.

But what if you find you're *not* a winning player—that even after you learn the game and put in some time studying and playing, you seem to be consistently losing or at best struggling to break even? Here are some suggestions:

- Play for the smallest stakes possible. Generally this will mean softer competition as well as limiting your losses.

- Purchase the practice software listed in Appendix C and confine yourself to battling computerized opponents. When you can beat the machine, you'll be ready for live play again.

- Investigate online poker forums (also described in Appendix C), where you can post sample hands and get a critique of your mistakes.

- Talk over your play with a friend, if possible. There's nothing like having to explain your strategy to bring mistakes to light.

- Rethink your goals. There's no shame in breaking even or losing small amounts if you can afford it. After all, people commonly set aside money for hobbies they enjoy.

- If you find yourself losing more than you can afford, or stealing time from other commitments to play Hold'em, seek help. Gambler's Anonymous, individual counseling, or trusted friends are all viable alternatives.

 Build Your Stack _____

> Even the best players don't do much better than one-and-a-half big bets per hour, and a win rate of two big bets per hour is considered phenomenal. It's generally easier to achieve a high win rate in low-limit and middle-limit games, where the competition is softest. At the higher limits, win rates drop despite the actual dollars being bigger. To take an example, a professional who can beat a $15-$30 game for 1.5 big bets per hour may be better off there than in a $20-$40 game he can beat for only one big bet per hour.

Protect Yourself with a Bankroll

Let's assume your records confirm that at your current level of stakes, it's plausible you're a winning player. What's the next step in coping with variance?

Simple enough. Essentially, if you play poker for any stakes above nickel-ante, you should set aside a set amount of money dedicated only to playing. In poker terms, this is called a *bankroll*.

Poker experts who are handy with statistics have come up with numbers to describe how big your bankroll should be to avoid going broke. In general, these numbers suggest that if you're playing limit poker and you're a winning player, you should start with a bankroll of 200 to 300 big bets. So for example if you're playing $3-$6 Hold'em at your local casino, you'd want a bankroll of $1,200 to $1,800 starting out.

This might seem like a lot of money to commit to what is just a hobby—and indeed, many recreational poker players avoid thinking in terms of a bankroll. They just pull money out of their pocket as they go along. But a bankroll is a far better approach. You'll feel more comfortable during losing streaks, and winning streaks won't get you as puffed up. And just as with your record-keeping, you'll always know where you stand.

If your bankroll starts growing, you'll have two choices: Either pull the money out as profit, or plow it back in. Plowing it back in will eventually allow you to move up to a higher limit, if that's your ambition. Either way you'll be in control.

Poker Time Vs. Life Time

Just a brief mention here: Along with good record-keeping and a bankroll, you should also use plain common sense to keep poker from rattling you. The best antidote for a losing streak is often to take a break. Even when winning, don't focus too much on the game; allow time in your life for family, friends, and other pursuits.

 Watch Your Chips

We suggest being especially careful about online poker: its constant availability makes it easy to get over-involved. You may want to set a schedule—for example, play a lot one week, then take the next week off. Or just play on weekends. However you do it, you'll have more fun and less frustration if you keep it fresh.

Turning Pro

This is a long shot, but it may happen: You steadily get better, until you find yourself sitting in middle-limit games and beating them. You've come to rely on the small income you generate from poker to pay for extras like a new computer or a vacation trip.

If this is the case, you can already regard yourself as a semi-professional player. As long as you keep a good balance, there's no reason you can't keep your day job and have some profitable fun on the side. There's not much more to say about that.

But what if it occurs to you that you enjoy poker *more* than your day job. Why not make it your real job, then? Playing the game you enjoy so much for a living—why not?

There are lots of reasons why not. Here are some of them:

- Remember variance? It's not impossible that you could enjoy several years of excellent results, only to discover you were statistically overachieving. Tales are rife in Las Vegas of technically unsound newcomers who skyrocketed for a year or two, then fizzled as their lack of fundamentals caught up to them.

- As countless pros have found before you, what's fun part-time can be brutal as a daily job. This applies especially to online play. Judging by posts on the online poker forums, legions of college students or recent grads, generally male, are attempting to make a go of it as online poker professionals. Only a very few will survive; the rest will exhaust themselves, then discover how far behind they've fallen in developing conventional job prospects.

- To succeed at high-stakes poker in particular, you've got to persuade yourself that the big stacks of money you're shoving onto the table are only good for gambling with. This cultivated indifference to money seems to get many big-time pros in trouble, as they periodically go broke or gamble their poker millions away on trivialities like sports betting.

- Think it's hard to get consumer credit as a writer, artist, or freelancer? Just try it if you list your occupation as "poker professional."

It's our opinion (and it's only an opinion) that Hold'em is better as a hobby or even a second job than as a full-time focus. However, we know of many full-time professionals who appear to lead successful and fulfilling lives. If you do find yourself winning steadily and can envision making Hold'em a rewarding career, you certainly won't be alone.

The Least You Need to Know

- Keep records of your playing sessions, using hours played, stakes, and wins and losses to calculate your average hourly rate.
- Create a poker bankroll to sustain you through times of hardship and plenty alike. To be safe, aim for a bankroll of 200 to 300 times the big bet at your current limit.
- Be wary of getting too hooked on poker—especially online poker—to the exclusion of other things in life.
- If you ever think about going pro, take a hard look at the potential liabilities and the soundness of your poker skills.

Hold'em Terminology

all-in To bet your last remaining chips on a hand, so that you have nothing left. More common in tournaments and *no-limit* than in *limit*.

angleshooting Unethical tricks and ploys designed to win the pot or gain an advantage for the angleshooter who uses them.

ante In poker in general, a bet required of all players before the first card is dealt. Hold'em is usually played with a special form of ante, called *blinds*.

aggressive Frequently betting or raising.

baby A small card, generally a six or lower.

backdoor A draw that requires two consecutive cards to hit. For example, a backdoor flush draw requires additional suited cards on both the turn and river.

bad beat An especially stinging defeat. Generally reserved for hands in which you were the presumptive favorite, but your opponent ignored the principles of sound play and got lucky.

bankroll Money reserved for playing poker. Used by smart players to protect against *variance*.

big blind See *blinds*.

Big Slick Nickname for AK. Also known as "Walking Back to Houston" for its propensity to *bust out* when no Ace or King flops.

blinds Blind bets required prior to cards being dealt. In *limit* Hold'em, the *little blind* or *small blind* can be from ⅓ to ⅔ the initial bet size. It is *posted* by the player one seat to the left of the *button*; the *big blind* is a full bet, and is posted by the player two seats to the left of the button.

board The currently displayed *community cards*, whether the flop alone, the flop plus turn, or the flop plus turn and river.

brick and mortar A casino, club, or other venue where live Hold'em games are offered, as opposed to online play.

bubble See *on the bubble*.

burn When dealing either the flop, turn, or river, the dealer first *burns* the top card in the deck by discarding it face-down, and only then deals the common cards. Intended to discourage cheating.

bust out Of *hole cards*: to lose by failing to connect in any way with the *board*. Of a player in a no-limit or tournament game: to lose all of one's chips and be forced to drop out.

button The marker (usually a plastic disk) that moves left with each deal, denoting the last player to act for that hand. Also shorthand for the player with the button: "The button raised."

buy-in Chips initially purchased when joining a Hold'em table.

call To match exactly the amount of a bet.

calling station A player who habitually calls when he should fold.

cash game A regular or nontournament poker game.

check To take no action when it's your turn to bet. Checking is only allowed in the absence of a bet on the table.

check-raise To check the first time the action comes to you, then raise if a player behind you bets.

chop In a casino game, if all players fold to the *blinds*, these two players can agree to chop, meaning each takes back his blind bet rather than play the hand out. This avoids paying the *rake*, which is generally high in low-stakes games and which would be especially onerous in a pot involving only two players.

community cards Those cards comprising the *flop*, *turn*, and *river*, which are shared by all players.

connected, connectors *Hole cards* adjacent in rank, such as 98.

counterfeit If you *flop* or *turn* a *flush* or *straight*, and a card comes on the next *street* which fails to improve your hand but makes possible a higher flush or straight for an opponent, you have been *counterfeited*.

cutoff A positional term, indicating the player to the immediate right of the player with the dealer *button*.

dealer The player with the *button*.

dealer button See *button*.

dominated If one hand has only three outs against another, that hand is said to be *dominated*. An example is AK and AQ. Excluding straights, the AQ has only the remaining three Queens as *outs* to win. All other cards, including an Ace, favor the AK.

draw Typically, a hand such as a straight or flush; to call a bet in hopes of making such a hand on the next card.

drawing hand See *draw*.

early position Relative to the dealer *button*, to be one of the first players required to act. Generally a disadvantage.

expectation In poker, a means of examining probabilities to determine whether a given play will make or cost you money in the long run. The former is *positive expectation*, the latter, *negative expectation*.

fish   A weak, losing player.

floor   A general term for cardroom managers.

flop   The first three common cards, followed by the *turn* and *river*.

flush   A five-card poker hand in which all five cards are of the same suit.

fold   To decline to call a bet or raise by discarding one's cards.

full house   A five-card poker hand comprised of three of a kind plus a pair.

good game   A game in which you can expect to make money from one or more very bad players.

hand   Used variously to mean either your hole cards, any five-card combination of your *hole cards* and the *community cards*, or any given deal of the cards.

head-up, heads-up   A hand limited to two players.

hole cards   The two private face-down cards held by every player. Also called *pocket* cards.

hourly rate   The average amount you make (or lose) for each hour of play. Usually measured both in dollars and in big bets for a given *limit*.

implied odds   A variation of *pot odds*, in which calling a relatively small bet now with a drawing hand gives you a chance of making that hand and collecting future bets of greater size.

jam To put in the maximum raises on any given *street*.

kicker If you pair one of your hole cards with a card on the *board*, your unpaired card is your kicker.

late position To be either the *dealer* or nearly so, and thus among the last to act on each betting round. Generally an advantage.

leak A flaw in your game that reduces your *expectation*.

limit Poker in which bets and raises are limited to a preset amount. Also refers to a given level of stakes. See also *no-limit* and *pot-limit*.

limp To play hole cards before the flop by calling the *big blind*, rather than raising.

little blind See *blinds*.

loose To play too many hands, call too many raises, and so on.

loose-aggressive A loose player who loves to bet and loves raising even more.

loose-passive A loose player who hates to bet and hates raising even more.

made hand The opposite of a drawing hand; a hand that doesn't need to improve to be a possible winner. Examples include big *pocket* pairs and high pairs made by pairing the *board*.

mathematical expectation See *expectation*.

middle position Relative to the dealer *button*, to be among neither the first nor the last players required to act.

muck To fold hole cards by discarding them face down in the direction of the dealer. Also a noun referring to the existing heap of discarded cards.

negative expectation See *expectation*.

no-limit Poker in which no limit is placed on the size of raises or bets, up to the amount of chips or cash a player has on the table.

nuts The best possible hand as determined by the *community cards*. Note that each new community card can redefine the nuts.

odds A ratio expressing the chances of a desired event occurring. In the case of poker, this event is either winning the pot (with no more cards to come) or drawing a card that improves your hand to the winner (with exactly one card to come). See also *pot odds*, *implied odds*, *reverse implied odds*, and *outs*.

offsuit Unsuited hole cards.

on the bubble In tournaments, players struggling to keep from getting eliminated and who are only a slot or two away from sharing in the prize money are said to be *on the bubble*.

open To begin the betting on a particular *street*.

open-ended A straight draw with eight outs, the maximum. An example would be holding hole cards of JT on a flop of 98x: any of the four Sevens or four Queens would make you a straight.

outs Cards that can improve your hand on the turn or river.

overbet In *no-limit*, to bet an amount larger than the pot.

overcards Hole cards higher in rank than any *community cards*.

passive Rarely betting or raising. Generally a losing approach to poker.

play back To respond aggressively to a bet or raise by raising back in return.

pocket See *hole cards*.

position Your seat relative to the *button*. In Hold'em, position determines who acts first. All things being equal, the later your position, the more information you have and the greater your advantage over players who must act before you.

positive expectation See *expectation*.

post To make a blind bet, e.g. "He posted the *big blind*."

pot-limit Poker in which bets and raises are limited to the size of the pot. This allows the pot to grow geometrically.

pot odds In poker, the ratio of the pot you hope to win versus the total bet you must call. Usually compared to odds.

pre-flop Shorthand for all action occurring before the *flop*.

quads   Four of a kind, such as KKKK.

raise   As a verb, to bet an additional amount over and above the current bet; as a noun, a bet that increases the current bet.

rake   That portion of the pot taken by the casino as its way of making money from a poker game.

redraw   The possibility of improving a strong made hand by catching a card that makes it even stronger, and thus beating a drawing hand that had temporarily improved to beat you.

reverse implied odds   A situation wherein you flop a made hand such as top pair, but face many opponents with good drawing hands. Most of the cards that can come will help them and do nothing for you, so your chances of winning only get worse.

ring game   Any game with seven or more players. Most Hold'em advice pertains to ring games, as opposed to *short-handed* games.

river   The fifth and final *community card*.

run over   To win money from a timid opponent by playing extra-aggressively, often with bluffs and unorthodox raises.

second pair   The second-highest pair on a particular flop or board.

semi-bluff   To bet or raise with a drawing hand in hopes that your opponent may fold, knowing that even if he doesn't, you may still win if your hand improves.

set   Three of a kind made by holding a pocket pair which matches one community card. See *trips*.

short-handed   Any game with six or fewer players. Short-handed games require a different strategy than *ring games*.

showdown   The revealing of players' hands after all betting has been concluded on the river. Only required if more than one player is still in.

small blind   See *blinds*.

spread limit   A form of *limit* poker in which bets may be any amount between a stated minimum and maximum. Raises must be at least the amount of the previous bet. For example, if a player makes an initial bet of $2, you can raise to make the total bet anywhere from $4 to $5 ($4 plus $4, or $4 plus $3), but not $3 ($2 plus $1).

stack   The amount of chips a player has in front of him or her.

straddle   A blind raise allowed by most casinos and clubs, in which the player *under the gun* posts a raise before the cards are dealt.

straight   A five-card poker hand in which all five cards are consecutive in rank.

street   The current betting round. In Hold'em, the streets are *pre-flop*, *flop*, *turn*, and *river*.

structured limit   A form of *limit* poker in which bets and raises must be a fixed amount. For Hold'em, the limit typically doubles on the turn. Common structured limits are $2-$4, $3-$6, $5-$10, $10-$20, and so on.

suited   Two *hole cards* of the same suit.

suited trash   Suited hole cards too far apart in rank to make a straight—for example, J3s or 92s.

tainted outs   Cards dealt during the *flop, turn,* or *river* that can improve your hand, but may improve an opponent's hand more. For example, if you have a straight draw and an opponent has a flush draw, two of your outs will be of his suit and thus tainted. See *outs.*

tight   The opposite of loose: a player who folds most of his hole cards, calls few raises, and so on.

tilt   To play badly when upset or angry; often occurs after a *bad beat.*

tell   An unintentional physical betrayal by a player of the quality of his hand or of his intentions. Includes mannerisms, tone of voice, posture, facial expressions, etc.

top pair   The best pair made possible by the current *board.*

trash hand   A hand of such irredeemably low quality that it should generally be folded rather than played.

trips   Three of a kind. In Hold'em, this generally refers to three of a kind made with one of your hole cards and two *community cards.*

turn   The fourth *community card,* coming after the flop and before the river.

two pair   A five-card poker hand made up of two different pairs and an unrelated card.

under the gun Before the flop, to be the first player to act—that is, the first player seated to the left of the blinds.

variance The semi-random fluctuations in a poker player's wins and losses over time.

weak-tight Prone to folding all but the very best hands.

Hold'em Odds Tables

The following tables assume you're familiar with the concepts of drawing odds and counting your outs, in the form of cards that can improve your hand. If you need to, review Chapter 3.

Odds for Flopping Good with Various Hole Cards

These odds are interesting, but not vital to memorize. It's worth noting that the odds of flopping a straight draw, flush draw, or set are considerably worse than the odds of flopping a pair when holding two big cards. This is one reason why you want more company with drawing hands such as small pairs and suited connectors.

Note also that we didn't list the full range of possibilities. For example, if you hold AK, there are many additional hands you can flop that are better than a single pair—two pair, a straight, a full house, a backdoor flush draw, and so on.

Odds for Flopping Good with Various Hole Cards

Hand	Example	Desired hand	Percent	Odds Against
Pocket pair	AA	Set	10.8%	8.3 to 1
Big cards	AK	Pair	29%	2.5 to 1
Suited cards	A3s	Flush draw	11%	8.1 to 1
Offsuit connectors	98	Straight draw	11.8%	7.5 to 1
Suited connectors	JTs	Straight or flush draw	16%	5 to 1

Odds from Flop to Turn

What are the chances your hand will improve on the flop by seeing one more card—namely, the turn?

To read this table, first count your outs in the left-hand column, before looking at your percent change of improving and the odds against doing so. Note that although we include percentages for the sake of completeness; in practice you'll think mostly in terms of odds and outs.

Odds from Flop to Turn

Outs	Percent	Odds to 1	Example
15	31.9	2.1	Straight flush draw, drawing to either a straight or flush
14	29.8	2.4	
13	27.7	2.6	
12	25.5	2.9	
11	23.4	3.3	
10	21.3	3.7	Set, drawing to a full house or quads
9	19.1	4.2	Flush draw
8	17.0	4.9	Straight draw
7	14.9	5.7	

continues

Odds from Flop to Turn (continued)

Outs	Percent	Odds to 1	Example
6	12.8	6.8	Straight draw versus flush draw; also over-cards, drawing to top pair
5	10.6	8.4	Pair using board card, drawing to trips or two pair
4	8.5	10.8	Inside straight draw; also two pair, drawing to a full house
3	6.4	14.7	
2	4.3	22.5	Pocket pair, drawing to a set

Odds from Turn to River

Again, you're seeing just one card here, but this time it's the river card. These odds are almost identical to the odds for drawing one card on the flop, so if you want to, you can just remember one set of odds or the other.

Odds from Turn to River

Outs	Percent	Odds to 1	Example
15	32.6	2.1	Straight flush draw, drawing to either a straight or flush
14	30.4	2.4	
13	28.3	2.5	
12	26.1	2.8	
11	23.9	3.2	
10	21.7	3.6	Set, drawing to a full house or quads
9	19.6	4.1	Flush draw
8	17.4	4.8	Straight draw
7	15.2	5.6	
6	13.0	6.7	Straight draw versus flush draw; also overcards, drawing to top pair
5	10.9	8.2	Pair using board card, drawing to trips or two pair
4	8.7	10.5	Inside straight draw; also two pair, drawing to a full house
3	6.5	14.3	
2	4.3	22.0	Pocket pair, drawing to a set

Odds from Flop to River

Let's say you plan to see *both* the turn and river in your quest to improve.

You're seeing two cards rather than just one—so shouldn't your odds be twice as good? In fact, they're not. The answer is complicated from a mathematical standpoint, but you can take our word for it that the following table reflects your true percentages and odds for a two-card draw.

Odds from Flop to River

Outs	Percent	Odds to 1	Example
15	54.1	0.8*	Straight flush draw, drawing to either a straight or flush
14	51.2	1.0	
13	48.1	1.1	
12	45.0	1.2	
11	41.7	1.4	
10	38.4	1.6	Set, drawing to a full house or quads
9	35.0	1.9	Nut flush draw
8	31.5	2.2	Straight draw
7	27.8	2.6	

Outs	Percent	Odds to 1	Example
6	24.1	3.1	Straight draw versus flush draw; also over-cards, drawing to top pair
5	20.3	3.9	Pair using board card, drawing to trips or two pair
4	16.5	5.1	Inside straight draw; also two pair, drawing to a full house
3	12.5	7.0	
2	8.4	10.9	Pocket pair, drawing to a set

* *You're a 1.2-to-1 favorite.*

Appendix C

Poker Resources

Once you've read the covers off this book and played a few hundred hours of Hold'em, you'll be ready for more advanced information. Toward that end, here are some books, online resources, and software to help you hone your skills.

Recommended Books

Sklansky, David and Mason Malmuth. *Hold'em Poker for Advanced Players*, Two Plus Two Publishing, 1999.

If you aspire to playing limit Hold'em at limits from $15-$30 and upward, this is the book for you. The authors assume you already know how to play the game well, so be warned: without a great deal of experience, you'll find what they say more confusing than helpful. Topics covered include short-handed play, reading opponents, and semi-bluffing.

Miller, Ed. *Small Stakes Hold'em: Winning Big with Expert Play*, Two Plus Two Publishing, 2004.

A fabulous advance in the literature of Hold'em, concentrating on beating loose games full of terrible opponents. Games have become increasingly easy to find not just at low limits, but at mid-limits. The only down side is that Miller is writing well over the heads of beginners, to the point that they could get into trouble if they try to follow his advice without grasping the nuances. Written in conjunction with long-time poker authorities Mason Malmuth and David Sklansky.

Cooke, Roy and John Bond. *Real Poker: The Cooke Collection*, Mike Caro University, 1999.

A collection of columns originally written for *Card Player Magazine*. Roy Cooke is one of those rare poker writers who admits to being human and making mistakes; on the other hand, he's a heck of a good Hold'em player. The combination makes this book both entertaining and highly instructive. Some of the columns focus strictly on how a top Hold'em player makes his technical decisions at the table. Others address less technical, but equally critical subjects, such as self-knowledge and emotional control.

Brunson, Doyle. *Doyle Brunson's Super System*, Cardoza Publishing, 1979.

One of the most venerated poker books of all time, now available in paperback. Much of the advice has been rendered out-of-date, but the no-limit Hold'em section is still required reading if that's your game: Brunson was a monster at no-limit, winning the World Series of Poker no-limit championship in 1976 and 1977. He later admitted to regretting giving away so many of his secrets in *Super System*.

McEvoy, Tom and Brad Daugherty. *No-Limit Texas Hold'em: The New Player's Guide to Winning Poker's Biggest Game*, Cardoza Publishing, 1989.

This fairly new book is by two respected tournament players, each of whom has won the no-limit Hold'em championship at the World Series of Poker. McEvoy and Daugherty walk you through a large number of example hands, in addition to clearly presenting the adjustments a limit player must make in moving to no-limit.

Sklansky, David. *The Theory of Poker*, by David Sklansky. Two Plus Two Publishing, 1989.

If you want a deeper understanding of poker in general, including but not limited to Hold'em, start here. Just be prepared to put in some serious study time! Sklansky may not have invented poker, but he has done more than any other writer to popularize a technical approach to winning. He may even have invented certain technical terms now in common use, for example, *implied odds*. The book is full of useful insights into improving your play, but it's not for the faint-hearted.

Burgess, Randy. *Stepping Up: The Recreational Player's Guide to Beating Casino and Internet Poker*, ConJelCo, 2003.

Okay, so one of us wrote this book (and the other provided some key input). But it's still a useful read for new players who've gotten comfortable enough with beginning Hold'em to work on acquiring more advanced skills. There are separate chapters on reading players and hands, identifying tells, avoiding strategic mistakes, taming tilt, and refining your game.

Online Resources

There are two popular spots on the Internet for discussing poker: One is a Usenet newsgroup, rec.alt.gambling, and the other is a web-based forum hosted by Two Plus Two Publishing, www.twoplustwo.com.

rec.alt.gambling is easy to get to, either from Google's Groups tab (just type in the name of the group you're interested in), or by setting up your e-mail client to read newsgroups.

What's not so easy is sorting through the ton of messages to find those that are interesting and/or useful. According to one source, rec.alt.gambling now gets more than 20,000 posts a month. And judging by a recent sample, many of these posts are off-topic or just plain spam. Unfortunately, a recent proposal for a moderated version of this newsgroup failed to gain enough support. It's still a great place to discuss poker, with a strong community feeling despite the junk posts.

www.twoplustwo.com, on the other hand, is definitely moderated! The forum is hosted by the same site used to advertise Two Plus Two Publishing's many poker books, so you're bombarded with advertising every time you visit. On the other hand, the discussions are lively and many of the posters are top-notch.

You can post your own hands for discussion at either place. Just be prepared for brutal honesty: your fellow posters won't hold back when educating you about your mistakes. You can also lurk— just read messages without posting—until you get comfortable with the setting.

Software

StatKing is a handy Windows program for keeping track of your poker results and calculating such neat stuff as your hourly rate and standard deviation (a measure of how big your swings are). It's available from ConJelCo, at www.conjelco.com.

If you play only online, you may want to skip StatKing and use PokerTracker instead. This program gets rave reviews from online players for its ability to import hand histories from most of the popular online sites and instantly presents you with statistics not for your own play, but for opponents as well. A free demo is available from www. pokertracker.com.

Wilson Software makes a variety of widely respected poker practice programs, including one for Hold'em called Turbo Texas Hold'em. Although the initial price of $90 or so may seem steep, it's a great way to get practice without losing money at the tables. See www.wilsonsoftware.com for more information.

Index

A

acting out of turn, 154
advanced lessons
    game types. *See* game
      types
    hand-reading
      common tells,
        122-123
      sample scenarios,
        120-122
    semi-bluffing, 108-110
    types of players,
      110-113
aggressive players, 59
    loose-aggressive
      players, 110
    short-handed play, 151
angleshooting tricks
    acting out of turn, 154
    looking at other
      player's cards,
      153-154
    lying about hands, 153
    shorting the pot, 153

B

bad beats, 103
bankrolls, 160-161
betting
    advantages of position,
      27
    before the flop, 23-25
    big blinds, 21-22
    casinos and clubs, 146
    little blinds, 21-22
    mistakes to avoid,
      95-96
    no-limit betting, 20,
      127-130
    on the flop, 25-26
    pot-limit, 21
    pre-flop hand selec-
      tion, 59-67
    raises. *See* raises
    river cards, 86-89,
      26-27
      calling bets, 88
      raising, 89
    spread limit betting,
      21
    structured limit bet-
      ting, 21
    table stakes, 146
    turn cards, 26-27, 83